ETHICS IN MANAGEMENT

RESEARCH IN ETHICAL ISSUES IN ORGANIZATIONS

Series Editors: Jacqueline Boaks, Michael Schwartz, Howard Harris

Recent Volumes:

Volume 20:	Applied Ethics in the Fractured State – Edited by Bligh Grant, Joseph Drew and Helen E. Christensen
Volume 21:	The Next Phase of Business Ethics: Celebrating 20 Years of REIO – Edited by Michael Schwartz, Howard Harris and Debra R. Comer
Volume 22:	Ethics in a Crowded World: Globalisation, Human Movement and Professional Ethics – Edited by Vandra Harris
Volume 23:	War, Peace and Organizational Ethics – Edited by Michael Schwartz and Howard Harris
Volume 24:	Educating for Ethical Survival – Edited by Michael Schwartz, Howard Harris, Charmayne Highfield and Hugh Breakey
Volume 25:	Transcendent Development: The Ethics of Universal Dignity – Edited by Andani Thakhati
Volume 26:	Who's Watching? Surveillance, Big Data and Applied Ethics in the Digital Age – Edited by Adrian Walsh and Sandy Boucher
Volume 27:	Social Licence and Ethical Practice – Edited by Hugh Breakey

RESEARCH IN ETHICAL ISSUES IN
ORGANIZATIONS   VOLUME 28

ETHICS IN MANAGEMENT: BUSINESS AND THE PROFESSIONS

EDITED BY

JACQUELINE BOAKS
Curtin University, Australia

United Kingdom – North America – Japan
India – Malaysia – China

Emerald Publishing Limited
Emerald Publishing, Floor 5, Northspring, 21-23 Wellington Street, Leeds LS1 4DL.

First edition 2025

Editorial matter and selection © 2025 Jacqueline Boaks.
Individual chapters © 2025 The authors.
Published under exclusive licence by Emerald Publishing Limited.

Reprints and permissions service
Contact: www.copyright.com

No part of this book may be reproduced, stored in a retrieval system, transmitted in any form or by any means electronic, mechanical, photocopying, recording or otherwise without either the prior written permission of the publisher or a licence permitting restricted copying issued in the UK by The Copyright Licensing Agency and in the USA by The Copyright Clearance Center. Any opinions expressed in the chapters are those of the authors. Whilst Emerald makes every effort to ensure the quality and accuracy of its content, Emerald makes no representation implied or otherwise, as to the chapters' suitability and application and disclaims any warranties, express or implied, to their use.

British Library Cataloguing in Publication Data
A catalogue record for this book is available from the British Library

ISBN: 978-1-83662-575-9 (Print)
ISBN: 978-1-83662-574-2 (Online)
ISBN: 978-1-83662-576-6 (Epub)

ISSN: 1529-2096 (Series)

INVESTOR IN PEOPLE

CONTENTS

About the Editor — *vii*

About the Contributors — *ix*

KEYNOTE

Chapter 1 Research Ethics for Social Impact
Michelle Greenwood and Margaret Ying Wei Lee — *3*

CONFERENCE PAPERS

Chapter 2 The Ethics of Passion at Work: Definition and Critique
Ezechiel Thibaud — *19*

Chapter 3 Three Types of Social Licence to Operate: The Ethical and Operational Risks of Authentic, Deceptive, and Default SLO Approaches
Hugh Breakey, Graham Wood and Charles Sampford — *39*

Chapter 4 Evaluative Consistency and Ethical Leadership
Jessica Flanigan — *57*

Chapter 5 Defending the Lives of Others: A Duty to Forcefully Intervene?
Shannon Brandt Ford — *73*

Chapter 6 How an Ethics of Care Can Transform Corporate Leadership: The Layered Round Table Approach
Larelle Bossi and Lonnie Bossi — *85*

BOOK REVIEWS

Chapter 7 Book Review: Martha Nussbaum's *Justice for Animals: Our Collective Responsibility*
Jacqueline Boaks — *111*

ABOUT THE EDITOR

Jacqueline Boaks teaches Ethics and Leadership to undergraduate, MBA, and Executive Educations students at Curtin University. She has a background in management, consultancy, and academia and previously taught Ethics and Leadership at the University of Western Australia, Notre Dame University, and Curtin University. She is Vice President of the Executive Committee of the Australian Association of Professional and Applied Ethics, the Founder of the WA Ethics Outside Philosophy group, and the Co-editor of *Leadership and Ethics* (Bloomsbury). She has published widely on democracy, ethics, and leadership.

She is Editor of the journal *Ethical Issues in Organisations* (Emerald) and serves on the editorial board of the journal *Philosophy of Management* (Springer).

Her current research areas include leadership, applied ethics, business ethics, and the question of dirty hands in leadership.

ABOUT THE CONTRIBUTORS

Larelle Bossi is a knowledge broker who works in a multi- and transdisciplinary intersection inclusive of a diverse range of stakeholders and data sets. She has been developing her brand of biocultural ethics which works well alongside ecofeminist theories and First Nations kinship worldviews. She has written on blue ecofeminism, fishing, the colonization and decolonization of oceans, social and cultural licenses to operate, place attachment, and ocean ethics. She is a Research Fellow at the Institute of Ethics, Law and Governance at Griffith University, working on the Blue Economy Cooperative Research Centre project. She has also been teaching, presenting, and consulting in ethical leadership, decision making, and cultural transformation across sectors.

Lonnie Bossi has had over 25 years of Senior Executive experience in the Tourism, Hospitality, and Entertainment sectors across the USA, Australia, and Asia. His experience extends to participating at conferences globally as both Presenter and Panellist, as well as participating in various Advisory Panels at both industry and governmental levels. His topics of presentation include marketing, communication, stakeholder engagement, and transformational leadership. His leadership experience includes multiple board and CEO roles, with the former in both corporate and public bodies. He has led material strategic and cultural change at an organizational level in both the USA and Australia, and was a valued Industry Advisor to Government during the COVID-19 pandemic. His success with cultural transformation through courageous leadership, led his operation to increase performance despite the removal of high value business initiatives, as an exemplar case study of applying the ethics of care and responsibility, in contradiction to industry norms, to materially outperform the market.

Hugh Breakey is Deputy Director and a Senior Research Fellow in Moral Philosophy at Griffith University's Institute for Ethics, Governance and Law, Law Futures Centre, Brisbane, Australia. His work spans the philosophical subdisciplines of political theory, normative ethics, applied philosophy, and legal theory. He has extensive experience in the application of ethical, legal, and political philosophy to a wide array of challenging practical fields, including institutional governance, integrity systems and corruption, climate change, sustainable tourism, peacekeeping, safety industries, resource and common property, professional ethics, and international law.

Jessica Flanigan is the Richard L. Morrill Chair in Ethics and Democratic Values at the University of Richmond, where she teaches Leadership Ethics, Ethical Decision Making in Healthcare, and Critical Thinking. Her research addresses the ethics of public policy, medicine, and business. In *Pharmaceutical Freedom* (Oxford University Press, 2017), she defends the rights of self-medication. In *Debating Sex Work* (Oxford University Press, 2019), she defends the decriminalization of sex work. She has also published in journals such as *Philosophical Studies*, *The Journal of Business Ethics*, *Leadership*, *The Journal of Moral Philosophy*, and the *Journal of Political Philosophy*. She is currently writing a book about the ethics of pregnancy and a book about language and ethics. She is a proponent of effective altruism.

Shannon Brandt Ford is Senior Lecturer in International Relations at Curtin University, where he is the Course Coordinator for the International Relations Major (B.A.) and the Master of International Relations and National Security programmes. He is also a Board Member for the International Society of Military Ethics and Faculty Affiliate with the Programme on Cybersecurity and Internet Governance at Indiana University. His research has been published in the Journal of Military Ethics, Journal of Cyber Policy, Quartz, The Conversation, and The Interpreter. His selected publications include: 'Ethical Exceptionalism and the Just War Tradition: Walzer's Instrumentalist Approach and an Institutionalist Response to McMahan's "Nazi Military" Problem' in the Journal of Military Ethics, 'Rights-based Justifications for Self-defense: Defending a Modified Unjust Threat Account' in the International Journal of Applied Philosophy, and 'Jus Ad Vim and the Just Use of Lethal Force Short-of-War' in the Routledge Handbook of Ethics and War.

Michelle Greenwood is Professor at Monash University, Australia. Her research is in critical business ethics, which she has developed conceptually and qualitatively in the areas of ethics and HRM/employment, critical approaches to stakeholder theory and CSR, organizational visuals, and technological mediations. She has published 70+ articles, book chapters, and books. She has an ongoing interest in the politics and ethics of academic publishing. She currently serves as Co-editor-in-Chief of the Journal of Business Ethics.

Margaret Ying Wei Lee is an Organizational Sociologist at Monash University, Australia. Her academic research centres on disturbing experiences of health and illness with a particular interest in narrative medicine. She has dedicated the last six years to understanding burnout, its fallout, and the possibilities for recovery. She is writing a narrative non-fiction book based on her doctoral research which explored the lived experience of burnout recovery in organizational settings. Prior to academia, she worked as a healthcare journalist at a national newspaper and as a health economist working with Federal Governments to secure funding for new medicines.

Charles Sampford topped politics, philosophy, and law at Melbourne, combining them in his Oxford DPhil (1986). As Griffith's Foundation Dean of Law (1991), he established the curriculum and research culture that, within 21 years, earned the Law School a QS global ranking of 43rd in the world. He was Foundation Director of the Key Centre for Ethics, Law, Justice and Governance

About the Contributors

in 1999 and Foundation Director of the Institute for Ethics, Governance and Law (a joint initiative of the United Nations University, Griffith, QUT, and ANU) since 2004. He has written over 150 articles and chapters and 32 books and edited collections. In 2008, for his work on ethics and integrity systems, he was recognized by the ARC as one of the 20 researchers across all disciplines who had had the greatest impact. He was Convenor of the ARC Governance Research Network (2004–2010).

Ezechiel Thibaud is a Lecturer at the Education University of Hong Kong, where she teaches Philosophy and Education Theory for the Department of International Education. She holds a master's degree in Philosophy from the University of Bordeaux, and a Ph.D. in Philosophy from Lingnan University in Hong Kong. She is primarily interested in ethics, philosophy of education, and philosophy of technology. Her current interests include business and work ethics, AI in education and tech-solutionism, and the philosophy of internet trends.

Graham Wood is a Philosopher in the School of Humanities at the University of Tasmania located in Launceston. He is a member of the EthicsLAB (UTAS) and the Centre for Marine Socioecology (UTAS/CSIRO). His areas of research include sustainability, environmental philosophy, moral psychology, and cognitive science of religion. His research concerns the relationship between human values and a scientific understanding of the human condition. He examines this relationship within three realms: environmental philosophy, moral psychology, and cognitive science of religion. In his research, environmental, moral, and religious values are examined using insights from philosophy of mind, cognitive science, and evolutionary psychology.

KEYNOTE

CHAPTER 1

RESEARCH ETHICS FOR SOCIAL IMPACT

Michelle Greenwood and Margaret Ying Wei Lee
Monash Business School, Monash University, Australia

ABSTRACT

This chapter addresses the question of how might research ethics be conceptualised for social impact. *In response, we posit that ethics in research should not be confined to considerations of* processes *but be extended to the* objectives *and the* implicit choices *of the research, and the researcher's role in shaping these. Put differently, we seek to broaden the conceptualisation of research ethics beyond institutional compliance by arguing that researchers have a responsibility to consider the implications of the knowledge they create and need to turn a critical eye to the implicit assumptions that underpin their practice. This argument is developed through a public health exemplar that examines the link between HIV treatment and labour productivity for a cohort of tea plantation workers in Kenya. We begin by outlining the research programme, undertaken by a group of Boston University scholars, and then develop a framework for a broader view of research ethics. We evaluate the case of HIV+ tea workers in Kenya using this framework and elaborate a thesis for future ethical research practice.*

Keywords: Research ethics; research impact; institutional review boards; IRB; research framework

INTRODUCTION

This chapter addresses the question of *how might research ethics be conceptualised for social impact*. Research impact – understood as 'the contribution that research makes to the economy, society, environment or culture, beyond the contribution to academic research' (Australian Research Council, 2023) – has become a top priority for governments and universities and has significant implications for how we understand the responsibilities and ethics of academic research. Yet, to date, there is little explicit connection made between research impact and research ethics. This may be explained in part by the institutional focus of research ethics, primarily institutional review boards (IRB), being on the process rather than the content of the research.

Conventionally, research ethics have focussed on research processes and thus been understood in terms of researcher institutional compliance and ethical conduct (see Fisher & Anushko, 2008), specifically in three key ways: research subject protection; research excellence; and researcher compliance. A direct result of the horrors of World War II, the first concern centres around the wellbeing of the human or animal 'subject' and ensuring adequate protections for those participating in research. Second, what is referred to as research excellence, a focus on the quality of the methods and the assurance of their validity and reliability, suggests a moral obligation to 'best practice' in the public interest. Finally, the third focusses on the behaviour of the researchers themselves and seeks to curtail deviant behaviour such as plagiarism and fraud.

In contrast, broader conceptions of research ethics have sought to also consider the beneficiaries of research, specifically, whose interests and values are being served in the content of the research and who is benefiting from its outcomes. Described as engaging in 'distribution fairness' (Dachler & Enderle, 1989, p. 597), this approach to research ethics is not just concerned with the methods of social science but also its contents. Importantly, this position recognises the competing interests that underlie social science knowledge production and therefore its political nature. A further challenge to this position is that, at the point of distribution, knowledge is already derivative of various implicit choices that structure its impact. Thus, Dachler and Enderle (1989) advocate for greater attention to the *implicit choices* made during the process of research that ultimately define and shape the way social problems are defined, the questions that are posed and subsequently, the knowledge that is generated and those that are able to profit from it.

Researchers long have been urged to turn a critical eye inwards, to ourselves and our practice, oft discussed under the concept of reflexivity (Guillemin & Gillam, 2004; Jeanes, 2017). In this chapter, we argue that the ethical practice of research necessitates a reflexivity that considers the implicit choices and values underlying our knowledge creation. We conceptualise reflexivity as critical (self-) reflection that seeks to make explicit the oft unspoken and unacknowledged structural, processual and individual assumptions underlying our research. Thus, in response to the question of *how might research ethics be conceptualised for social impact*, we posit that ethics in research should not only be confined to considerations of *processes* but be extended to the *objectives* and the *implicit choices* of the research, and the researcher's role in shaping these. In other words, we seek to broaden the conceptualisation of research ethics beyond institutional compliance by arguing that researchers have a responsibility to consider the implications of the knowledge they create and need to turn a critical eye to the implicit assumptions that underpin their practice. We are not aiming to add to the *formal* research ethics processes that universities operate but are instead directing researchers' attention and consideration to the other areas that they morally should attend to more informally. This argument is developed through a public health exemplar that examines the link between HIV treatment and labour productivity for a cohort of tea plantation workers in Kenya. We begin by outlining the research programme undertaken by a group of Boston University scholars and then develop a framework for a broader view of research ethics. We evaluate the case of HIV+ tea workers in Kenya using this framework and elaborate a thesis for future ethical research practice.

EXEMPLAR CASE AND QUESTIONS ARISING

In an article published in Boston University's alumni publication *Bostonia* (Rolbein, 2010), significant research choices made by a team of Boston University public health researchers involved in a high-stake research investigation exploring the efficacy of antiretroviral therapy (ART) on tea workers in Kenya are exposed.

> The BU team [were] provided an opportunity to answer a crucial question: do workers who receive antiretroviral therapy return to full strength? If the answer were yes, it could persuade owners of tea plantations and perhaps other endeavors to treat their HIV-infected workers earlier, and better. But what if the answer were no? (Rolbein, 2010, p. 34)

Depending on the outcome of their research, employers may or may not continue to pay for this expensive life-saving drug treatment. The research team published three articles from these data and it is from these artefacts – the three published Larson et al. (2008, 2009, 2013) papers and *Bostonia* profile – that we have excavated the exemplar. We provide this case in the genre of clinical cases; that is, 'descriptive studies that are prepared for illustrating novel, unusual, or atypical features identified in ... practice, and they potentially generate new research questions' (Sayre et al., 2017, p. 1; see also Mir & Greenwood, 2021).

Since the onset of the epidemic in the 1980s, therapeutic developments, rapid testing and early access to treatment have rendered HIV a manageable chronic health condition (World Health Organization (WHO), 2016). However, HIV was and remains expensive to treat using ART, which not only suppresses the virus within the patient and halts progression to AIDS, but also prevents its transmission to other individuals (Roser & Ritchie, 2018). ART is most effective when initiated early and requires individuals to be on lifelong treatment (WHO, 2016). Thus, outcomes for people living with HIV differ significantly across resource settings. In sub-Saharan Africa, HIV remains the leading cause of morbidity and mortality due to constrained access to ART (Danforth et al., 2017), with the exemplar setting of Kenya having the fourth largest worldwide HIV epidemic (UNAIDS Joint United Nations Programme on HIV/AIDS, 2010).

It is against this backdrop of healthcare inequality that researchers from Boston University undertook a programme of research beginning in 2001 that began as

> an effort to measure the devastating impact of AIDS on African workers has evolved into something much more hopeful: an attempt to prove that HIV-infected workers, given the same antiretroviral drugs readily available in developed countries, will return to near full productivity, benefiting their employers as well as their families. (Rolbein, 2010, p. 32)

By analysing the relationship between ART and labour productivity the researchers were effectively hoping to present a 'business case' for employer-sponsored HIV treatment in Kenya. Three studies formed a part of this longitudinal research programme that was subject to design refinements over the various study periods (see Table 1.1).

Methodologically, the studies were cohort-based – as distinct from experimental methods – meaning all participants were observed in a 'real world' setting and were not exposed to a predetermined intervention, and relied on secondary data of varying quality. For example, existing employment records were used to extract productivity measures, however, employee identification numbers were sometimes reassigned meaning that individual-level outcomes experienced at least some level of confounding.

Of interest to the current discussion are the researchers' design refinements and the thinking behind these choices: specifically, the decision to stratify outcomes based on sex in the later studies; the addition of productivity measures in later studies; and changes in key motivators as indicated in the studies objectives and conclusions (see Table 1.1). To begin, in the first preliminary study, the objective was to estimate the impact of ART to '*to assess the potential economic benefits* of providing treatment to working adults' using an outcome measure of days spent plucking per month with no gender sampling (Larson et al., 2008, p. 421, my emphasis). The authors expressed their awareness that tea plantation owners 'have long understood that health care benefits the workers and improves the bottom line' (Rolbein, 2010, p. 34).

The second main study continued to explore the same phenomenon but with a shift in emphasis to 'the *socio-economic impacts* of ART' studying 'the extent to which improvements in health resulting from ART *allows individuals to return to work and earn income*' (Larson et al., 2009, p. 1, my emphasis). Importantly additional outcome measures were added to this study that examined days spent on non-plucking assignments and average output on days when plucking, which thus broadened the construct of productivity. Unlike the first study, this study sampled and reported men and women separately, with results showing 'a troubling gender disparity' (Rolbein, 2010, p. 35) that after ART women, but not men, were less productive compared with the reference group (Larson et al., 2009; see Table 1.1).

The third longitudinal follow-up study stated its objective as 'To estimate the impact of ART on *labor productivity and income*'. An additional measure of 'total income from labour per month' was added to the design, expanding the emphasis

Research Ethics for Social Impact

Table 1.1 Comparative Table of the Three Studies.

Study	Index Group[a] M/F	Reference Group M/F	Outcomes Measures	Study Objective/ Background (*Direct Quotations, Our Emphasis*)	Study Conclusion (*Direct Quotations, Our Emphasis*)
Preliminary study (Larson et al., 2008)	59 (no M/F)	1,992 (no M/F)	(i) Days spent plucking tea per month	Objective: This chapter estimates the impact of ART on days harvesting tea per month for tea-estate workers in Kenya. Such information is needed *to assess the potential economic benefits* of providing treatment to working adults	Treatment had a *large, positive impact on the ability of workers* to undertake their primary work activity, harvesting tea, in the first year on ART
Main study (Larson et al., 2009)	41M 56F	1,691M 794F	(i) Days spent plucking tea per month (ii) Days spent on non-plucking assignments per month (iii) Average daily output when plucking per month	Background: As access to ART has grown in Africa, attention has turned to evaluating the socio-economic impacts of ART. One key issue is the extent to which improvements in health resulting from ART *allows individuals to return to work and earn income*. Improvements in health from ART may also be associated with reduced impaired presenteeism, which is the *loss of productivity* when an ill or disabled individual attends work but accomplishes less at his or her usual tasks or shifts to other, possibly less valuable, tasks	*Significant impaired presenteeism* continued to exist among the *female* index group after one year on ART. Future research needs to explore further the *socio-economic implications of HIV-infected female workers on ART being less productive* than the general female workforce over sustained periods of time
Longitudinal follow-up, 24 months (Larson et al., 2013)	125M 112F	500M 448F	(i) Days spent plucking tea per month (ii) Days spent on non-plucking assignments per month (iii) Average daily output when plucking per month (iv) Total income from labour per month	Objective: To estimate the impact of (ART) on *labour productivity and income* using detailed employment data from two large tea plantations in western Kenya for HIV infected tea pluckers who initiated ART	HIV-infected workers experienced *long-term income reductions* before and after initiating ART. The implications of such *long-term impacts in low-income countries* have not been adequately addressed

[a] Index group refers to tea pluckers who received ART and reference group refers tea pluckers who did not receive ART and may or may not have had HIV.

on worker income. Furthermore, the conclusion shifts the focus not only to the impact on workers, but also the impact on society: 'HIV-infected workers experienced *long-term income reductions* before and after initiating ART. The implications of such *long-term impacts in low-income countries* have not been adequately addressed'.

It would appear that arising from changes in research design and measures, the research shifted from being concentrated on economic benefits to the company to being concerned with the impact on workers and society. We would suggest that this shift was influenced, at least in part, by choices made by the researchers; choices that need to be made 'when facing ethical dilemmas "in the moment" that require an immediate and personal response and cannot be codified' (Jeanes, 2017, p. 174).

Several key questions around the research choices relating to the research programme might be valuable to examine: first, there are questions that relate to *what is assumed about the status of the knowledge created* and, in particular, what is the link between the research findings and the 'truth' and what role do values play in the creation of facts? When explaining their study design to *Bostonia*, the researchers engaged in some debate regarding the impact of the stratified analysis in their main study, which showed that female workers were not returning to productivity as quickly as the men on all measures. While acknowledging the disturbing nature of the findings, their eventual response as stated in the article was to 'let the data speak' (Rolbein, 2010, p. 34).

Second, there are questions that relate to *what is assumed about the status of the researcher* and, in particular, what is the relationship between the researcher and the 'subject' and what is the role of critical reflection? In order to conduct a research programme of this scale, the researchers formed a long-term and purportedly 'mutually beneficial' relationship with stakeholders in Kenya (Rolbein, 2010). In their published work, however, they are cast as objective outsiders without situational relationships with the individuals involved.

We will explore these questions by first reconceptualising the horizons of research ethics through a framework for ethical research practice, then apply this framework to the ethics of this study of Kenyan tea pluckers and finally discuss the framework and its implication.

A FRAMEWORK FOR RESEARCH ETHICS FOCUSSED ON SOCIAL IMPACT

Dismantling the implicit assumptions of ethical orthodoxy brings us to the question of *how might research ethics be conceptualised for social impact*. To answer this, we develop a framework of approaches to research ethics by synthesising the 'implicit choice' view of ethics, noted earlier, advocated by Dachler and Enderle (1989) and Brewis and Wray-Bliss (2008) tripartite conceptualisation of research ethics: ethics as hurdle; ethics as seeking out silences; and ethics as central. We advance three approaches to research ethics (see Table 1.2) – a compliance approach, a stakeholder approach and a relational approach – and use this framework to critically assess the exemplar of tea plantation workers in Kenya.

Table 1.2 A Framework for Research Ethics Focussed on Social Impact

	Compliance Approach	Stakeholder Approach	Relational Approach
Primary focus on	Research process; that is, conduct of the research • protection of the subject • professional practice	Research content; that is, research objectives • values and interests served • who benefits (distribution fairness)	Implicit choices in research practice; that is, research problem, methods and outcomes and the implicit assumptions which underpin these • knowledge as negotiated • researcher reflexivity
Research priorities	All research interests are equally valid	Some research interests and outcomes are more important than others	Outcomes must be useful to the participants
Researcher as	An expert who seeks to know	An expert who seeks to know the position of the stakeholder	An interpreter who co-constitutes knowledge
Subject as	A research respondent who should be interfered with as little as possible	A respondent with a stake in the research outcome	A participant who co-constitutes knowledge
'Ethical' research as	'Ethical' practices such as IRB approval, informed consent, anonymity, open and transparent methods, honesty in data collection and analysis and declaration at publication	Research that focusses on value and meaning of consequences for (vulnerable) stakeholder/s	Research in which responsibility is taken for implicit choices (in the process of generating knowledge) as these choices are understood as constructing the value and meaning of consequences for stakeholder/s

The first idea, ethics from a *compliance approach*, speaks to the codified nature of ethical practice in research institutions. This view, which largely remains the convention for research organisations, conceives of ethics at best as a requirement to protect research subjects and uphold professional conduct and at worst as an obstruction to be overcome until the 'real' work of the research can be achieved. While this regulatory approach has a vital imperative, it also reduces the work of ethics to procedural compliance and lulls researchers into a false equivalence that conflates adherence to protocol with ethical conduct. In other words, relegating ethics to bureaucratic compliance neglects the critical issue of social praxis, that is, the spirit of ethical *conduct*. Specifically, the nature of institutional protocols is necessarily broad and therefore cannot be universally applied to the vagaries and complexities of individual research contexts. Take, for example, interpretations of a key ethical concept, anonymity. Protections for privacy and confidentiality are imperative to ethical research practice, however, should the research process uncover incidents of abuse, conventional frameworks and principles are likely to be limited in guiding how researchers should respond (see Guillemin & Gillam, 2004, for an extended discussion of such a scenario).

The second position frames ethics from a *stakeholder approach*. In this, the researcher extends their efforts beyond codified protocol and recognises the 'silencing' nature of the research process and the texts it produces. Financial resources (e.g. industry grants) and institutional arrangements (e.g. rewards for certain publications) invariably affect research choices and subsequent research outputs. Instead, researchers are encouraged to turn their attention to the *content* of their inquiry and seek to provide a 'voice' beyond the sectional interests of (research) institutions. By clarifying and making explicit the value base of the various stakeholders involved in the production of academic knowledge, and privileging certain stakeholders' interests (e.g. research participants) over others, researchers can seek 'distributive fairness' on behalf of vulnerable stakeholders (Dachler & Enderle, 1989, p. 598). Researchers that practice this approach to ethics, however, can (unknowingly) deprive participants of their agency and reproduce the lofty status of the researcher as 'agentic, superior knower' (Brewis & Wray-Bliss, 2008, p. 1531). Acknowledging that vulnerable groups still retain agency and legitimacy is key to mitigating this 'heroic researcher' archetype. Ultimately, this lens proposes an ethical obligation to not only collect and report on the experiences of those without equal pathways to power, but to also help practically change their situation.

The third lens extends this notion of the stakeholder approach to re-orient ethics with a *relational approach* to research. This conceptualisation recognises the relational nature of the research encounter and the intersubjectivity of morality that is created from the mutual exchange between the researcher and the researched. Significantly, its underlying tenet is that of collaborative research for a social good which benefits a *collective* of stakeholders, in particular those being researched. Effectively, this level of ethics seeks to balance or even blur the researcher/researched binary whereby the researched are transformed from the passive observed to partners in an ongoing research negotiation. This third lens of research ethics informs participatory approaches such as action research.

This framework of three approaches to research ethics is not intended to promote prescriptive and exclusive archetypes. It is the case that the different lenses, being linked as they are to implicit assumptions, vary in paradigmatic position. Yet, it is possible that any researcher/research project may see themselves in any, or indeed all, of these approaches and that all these approaches have their place. What is being advanced, however, is the argument that the third approach, a relational approach to research ethics, is intrinsically linked to social impact in a way that the others are not.

APPLYING THE FRAMEWORK: HIV, WORKER PRODUCTIVITY AND THE ETHICS OF IT ALL

Using this research ethics framework and the artefacts we have gathered – the three published papers by Larson et al. (2008, 2009, 2013) and their *Bostonia* profile (Rolbein, 2010) – we evaluate the ethics of the exemplar research programme.

First, when considering ethics as compliance, all three publications cite ethical reviews from a number of institutions: Boston University, the Kenya Medical Research Institute and the Walter Reed Army Institute for Research. This declaration – that invokes the credibility of major establishments – has the effect of assuring the reader of compliance with 'due process'. These ethical review statements have typically been a biomedical 'custom', whereby the institution and oftentimes the specific case identification number are cited in the discussion of methods, though in recent years this custom has started to bleed into social science and management journals. While a comforting addition, these declarations tell us very little about the real and practical means in which subjects have been protected, and begs the question: what constitutes 'adequate' protection during the research process and how can institutional procedures assist in providing these protections? A global study of editors of leading management journals (Greenwood, 2016) revealed that while ethical declarations were seen to be a largely accepted and beneficial practice, few journals (17%) actually required these statements in publication. The motivating reasons behind this practice were both practical as well as philosophical. Some editors suggested that ethical declarations could disincentivise author submissions, for example, by contributing to the increasing bureaucratisation of research and discriminating against authors who did not belong to institutions with an ethics review process. Most significantly, there was scepticism as to the effectiveness of these declarations in meaningfully providing protections for research participants both as individuals and as a collective subject. That is, by circumscribing morality and ethics to process-driven ethics committees, it absolves those who are actually *conducting* the research of personal responsibility to consider and act with morality. However, the indeterminate nature of social science research requires researchers to iteratively adjust their research design and continuously enact principles of morality and ethics, and as such, compliance-based measures are unlikely to meaningfully guarantee the wellbeing of participants, both individually and collectively. Rather, we posit that a focus on the objectives and implicit choices of research is more likely to perpetuate ethical behaviour as practitioners consistently reflect and act with the intention to uphold participants not only as individual 'respondents' but as a collective subject.

Next, we consider the research through the stakeholder approach. The researchers state in their 2013 publication that their purpose was to understand what they describe as the 'social effectiveness' of ART interventions in resource-limited settings. They describe the question they were trying to answer in *Bostonia* as: 'how do you measure the effects of illness in a workforce, real tangible effects on productivity, the bottom line, and people's lives, beyond simply absenteeism?' (Rolbein, 2010, p. 33). These statements that focus on broader measures of ART effectiveness in the developing world indicate that the researchers were at least considering extending 'pathways to power' for those affected by HIV, as do the reported team discussions. These discussions centred on the ethics of working with the private sector; the implications of the findings should they suggest prolonged impairment to productivity despite ART; and a reflection of their role as researchers. Ultimately, the research team concluded their interest in social activism should be confined to the 'off hours' and fundamentally, allow the data to 'speak' by 'very systematically collect[ing] information, present[ing] it in a fairly unvarnished way, and let the social policy decisions be informed' (Rolbein,

2010, p. 34). Superficially, this view of dislocated data gathering is reflected in the authors' narrow conception of social effectiveness in their 2008 and 2009 publications that focussed solely on labour productivity measures (see Table 1.1). A closer examination reveals, however, that despite avowed abstinence from social activism, the outcome of their 2008 preliminary study – which provided early evidence for the effectiveness of ART in improving productivity – sparked relief and was described as 'the results ... co-operating' (Rolbein, 2010, p. 35). This feeling of a 'weight having been lifted' and the subsequent evolution of the research design illustrate that, despite their best efforts, the research team was relationally engaged with the welfare of their participants, not only as individuals but as a collective whole.

The evolution of the research, from 2009 onwards, will be the focus of the third ethical lens, a *relational approach*. We argue that the steps taken by the researchers in this period do, in fact, place ethics as a relational endeavour. While these steps appeared to largely take place on an ad hoc basis and as a reactionary response to emergent concerns, we posit that these provide an unembellished example of collaborative research for social good. First, the relief experienced by the researchers in their preliminary study was short-lived. In their 2009 publication, Larson and colleagues expanded their sample population and stratified the analysis based on sex, justifying this with a brief allusion to the different gender-based roles in sub-Saharan Africa. What emerged from this analysis was characterised as a 'disturbing anomaly' (Rolbein, 2010). Specifically, the male index group was able to return to similar patterns of productivity as their reference cohort, however, the female index workers reported consistently lower levels of productivity on all measures after 12 months. This result, and its implications, perturbed the researchers and resulted in three key actions: (i) longitudinal follow-up for an additional 12 months, that is, 24 months in total post-ART initiation; (ii) the adoption of new matching methods of reference workers – in 2009, respondents were matched to the general workforce and in 2013, the researchers engaged in nearest neighbour matching on several potentially confounding characteristics: age; duration of employment; estate; calendar time and duration on ART; and (iii) introduction of a new welfare measure beyond productivity – income. While it is difficult to ascertain the intent behind these decisions, collectively, they provided an opportunity for the gender-based effects to smooth out over time using a broader definition of 'success'. The final publication in 2013 illustrates just this – the differences between the male and female index workers, while still present, had levelled out significantly over a 24-month period, for example, both were able to generate earnings similar to their reference groups (94% for men; 91% for women).

It can be said that these refinements simply constitute methodological improvements rather than moral behaviour. We refer to the artefacts to justify our assessment – the researchers did not passively 'let the data speak' as originally avowed, rather they sought to downplay and explain these gender-based differences in their published work as well in their *Bostonia* profile. For example, they cautioned against small sample sizes and introduced their cultural knowledge of life on the plantations suggesting that: 'the study size is small enough so that it might even be something as one foreman treating men and women differently [i.e. more compassionately assigning lighter work to women]. That can happen in field research like this' (Rolbein, 2010, p. 35). In addition, Larson and colleagues also engaged representatives of tea plantations, hospital staff and the Kenya Medical Research Institute in what we consider to be an (unconscious) attempt at participatory design. Specifically, they used this collaborative forum to 'crowdsource' feedback to explain the gender-based differences in their findings which also informed their subsequent methodological refinements. Another perspective might suggest that the methodological amendments are reminiscent of 'HARKING', otherwise known as 'hypothesising after results are known' which is typically considered a violation of the 'scientific' method of quantitative research. But such methodological worries do not appear to be in play here in any serious sense, since the researchers did not retrospectively amend their *initial* hypotheses. Instead, they returned to the data and conducted a further exploratory analysis based on *new* hypotheses – a practice reflective of standard scientific operating procedure that encourages iterative analysis in the face of anomalous findings. Ultimately, these new analytical avenues were able to provide an explanation for the initial gender-based disparities by taking into account composite outcome measures. From a relational perspective, an unwavering dedication to scientific convention without a social end represents a myopic view of research and its ethical constituents. As such, we regard the actions of Larson and colleagues, while seemingly impromptu, to be ethically and morally centred.

In summary, while Larson et al. (2008, 2009, 2013) have attempted to maintain conventional scientific practice across their research, it is clear that ethics has remained at the heart of their years-long research programme. While in this case, such considerations were largely ad hoc in nature, we argue that research practitioners should proactively and reflexively consider the welfare of their participants beyond codified practices and individual wellbeing, and consider the research encounter a mutual exchange between a collective subject and their own relationality.

DISCUSSION AND IMPLICATIONS

When faced with a high-stakes research investigation, the public health researchers from Boston University demonstrated actions indicative of a relational approach to research ethics. Earlier, we suggested that there were several key questions around the research choices relating to the research programme worthy of examination. First, there are questions that relate to *what is assumed about the status of the knowledge created* in particular what is the link between the research findings and the 'truth', and what role do values play in the creation of facts. Second, there are questions that relate to *what is assumed about the status of the researcher* in particular what is the relationship between the researcher and the 'subject', and what is the role of critical reflection. We will return to these questions and use them as a base to re-orientate to a relational approach to research ethics.

First, we explore the status of the knowledge created. Much social science research, with this public health exemplar being no exception, seeks truth in some form. From a relational viewpoint, researchers should be appropriately fallibilist and curious about outcomes. Ethically minded practitioners should recognise the dynamic nature of socially determined phenomena in which reality is never fixed and meaning is co-constructed. Acknowledging the fluid nature of social phenomena suggests that a singular notion of truth is both improbable and impractical and that facts are inherently revisable. In light of this, we suggest researchers re-orient their pursuits from seeking a 'definitive answer' to a 'best explanation' of the studied phenomena based on the knowledge and resources available at the time.

Related to the truth status of knowledge, is the underlying fact–value dichotomy. In this, 'facts' and 'values' are situated as oppositional and exclusionary concepts. Values contradict the 'detached observer' expectation of researchers and are thus considered to be flimsy and problematic in research practice. Facts, in being situated as the foil to values, are subsequently cast as weighty, credible and immutable. A relational view, however, disavows this notion of 'value-free' fact and suggests a more mixable intermingling of the two concepts. As interests and values are inherently embedded in the institutions that are charged with the formation of facts, facts thereby cannot be neutral. Thus, we consider it an ethical obligation of researchers to regard and understand facts in the context of their embedded values.

Second, we consider the status of the researcher. Much social science research, with this public health exemplar being no exception, assumes a lofty separation of the researcher and the researched 'subjects' in which the former occupies the position of an 'absent expert' who remains detached from the phenomena and those who experience it. The researcher in this view is considered an objective collector of data while remaining free from bias and opinion. The subjects, in contrast, are assumed to be passive and exist in isolation from the studied phenomena as well as the remaining aspects of their lives. In short, the practice and process of research is considered to be a closed entity in which the essential relatedness of individuals and the world around them is invalidated. We proffer that this is a naïve rendering of the social world; rather, individuals are intrinsically situated in complex and textured relationships and simply drawing a veil over these 'messy' realities does not invalidate the need for a more considered approach to their ethical implications. Instead, we suggest that ethical research practitioners need to reflexively acknowledge their relative subject positions, but also the inherent permeability between themselves and their research *participants*. We intentionally recast the role of 'subject' as 'participant' to recognise the reciprocal nature of the social research process in which a mutual exchange of humanity takes place. In other words, we suggest that in order to act ethically, researchers need to recognise the relational nature of themselves and their practice, and the potential for their research to create ongoing ripples in their lives and the lives of participants beyond the research encounter.

CONCLUSION

In order to conceptualise research ethics for social impact, we need to move beyond a compliance approach to ethics that focusses on research methods. Research content, with regard to values and outcomes, and the implicit choices that shape these values and outcomes must be brought front and centre. In examining the back story of a high-stakes public health study of HIV+ tea workers in Kenya, we expose a number of questions pertinent to the development of ethical research practice. Accordingly, we argue that a relational approach to research ethics that recognises the enmeshed nature of social knowledge and the critical role of researcher reflexivity provides a pathway to greater social impact.

REFERENCES

Australian Research Council. (2023). *Research impact principles and framework*. Australian Government. https://www.arc.gov.au/about-arc/strategies/research-impact-principles-and-framework

Brewis, J., & Wray-Bliss, E. (2008). Re-searching ethics: Towards a more reflexive critical management studies. *Organization Studies, 29*(12), 1521–1540.

Dachler, H. P., & Enderle, G. (1989). Epistemological and ethical considerations in conceptualizing and implementing human resource management. *Journal of Business Ethics, 8*(8), 597–606.

Danforth, K., Granich, R., Wiedeman, D., Baxi, S., & Padian, N. (2017). Global mortality and morbidity of HIV/AIDS. In K. K. Holmes, S. Bertozzi, B. R. Bloom, & P. Jha (Eds.), *Major infectious diseases* (p. 6). Washington (DC): The International Bank for Reconstruction and Development/The World Bank. https://www.ncbi.nlm.nih.gov/books/NBK525184/

Fisher, C. B., & Anushko, A. E. (2008). Research ethics in social science. In P. Alasuutari, L. Bickman, & J. Brannen (Eds.), *The Sage handbook of social research methods* (pp. 95–109). SAGE Publications Ltd.

Greenwood, M. (2016). Approving or improving research ethics in management journals. *Journal of Business Ethics, 137*(3), 507–520.

Guillemin, M., & Gillam, L. (2004). Ethics, reflexivity, and "ethically important moments" in research. *Qualitative Inquiry, 10*(2), 261–280.

Jeanes, E. (2017). Are we ethical? Approaches to ethics in management and organisation research. *Organization, 24*(2), 174–197.

Larson, B. A., Fox, M. P., Bii, M., Rosen, S., Rohr, J., Shaffer, D., Sawe, F., Wasunna, M., & Simon, J. L. (2013). Antiretroviral therapy, labor productivity, and sex: A longitudinal cohort study of tea pluckers in Kenya. *AIDS, 27*(1), 115–123. https://doi.org/10.1097/QAD.0b013e32835a5b12

Larson, B. A., Fox, M. P., Rosen, S., Bii, Sigei, C., Shaffer, D., Sawe, F., McCoy, K., Wasunna, M., & Simon, J. L. (2009). Do the socioeconomic impacts of antiretroviral therapy vary by gender? A longitudinal study of Kenyan agricultural worker employment outcomes. *BMC Public Health, 9*(1), 1–11.

Larson, B. A., Fox, M. P., Rosen, S., Bii, M., Sigei, C., Shaffer, D., Sawe, F., Wasunna, M., & Simon, J.L. (2008). Early effects of antiretroviral therapy on work performance: Preliminary results from a cohort study of Kenyan agricultural workers. *AIDS, 22*(3), 421–425.

Mir, R., & Greenwood, M. (2021). *Philosophy and management studies: A research overview*. Routledge.

Rolbein, S. (2010). What the tea leaves say. *Bostonia* (Winter-Spring), 30–35.

Roser, M., & Ritchie, H. (2018). *HIV/AIDS*. https://ourworldindata.org/hiv-aids

Sayre, J. W., Toklu, H. Z., Ye, F., Mazza, J., & Yale, S. (2017). Case reports, case series – From clinical practice to evidence-based medicine in graduate medical education. *Cureus, 9*(8), e1546.

UNAIDS Joint United Nations Programme on HIV/AIDS. (2010). Global report: UNAIDS report on the global AIDS epidemic. https://cir.nii.ac.jp/crid/1130282270037552256

World Health Organization (WHO). (2016). *Consolidated guidelines on the use of antiretroviral drugs for treating and preventing HIV infection: recommendations for a public health approach.* World Health Organization. https://www.ncbi.nlm.nih.gov/books/NBK374316/

CONFERENCE PAPERS

CHAPTER 2

THE ETHICS OF PASSION AT WORK: DEFINITION AND CRITIQUE

Ezechiel Thibaud

Department of International Education, The Education University of Hong Kong, Hong Kong

ABSTRACT

This chapter looks at the increasing role that passion plays in organizations, illustrated in particular through the Passion Economy, *by Adam Davidson (2020a). This book argues that Western economies are shifting from a sacrifice-based model of work to a passion-based one. Generally, the importance of passion for work is further and further emphasized, as more and more workers and companies look to boost motivation and create more meaning in the workplace. This chapter describes the way passion is often seen as a response to contemporary work-related ills, but argues that despite some benefits, passion fails to present a robust measure of success at work and runs the risk of elitism. The author worries that the focus on passion could cause harm to workers, by detracting organizations from the goal of improving work conditions in a sustainable way, especially for workers who may never have a passion-driven career.*

Keywords: Passion; work; ethics; economy; workplace conditions

INTRODUCTION

The effects of passion for work on workers, and its benefits for organizations, have been increasingly discussed (Cabrita & Duarte, 2023; Lavigne et al., 2014; Vallerand & Houlfort, 2019). From its supposed motivational effects to the hope that it might boost productivity and innovation, the consensus seems to be that passion for work is a desirable quality (Pollack et al., 2020). It is often regarded as an essential feature that employers look for when hiring new staff (Polson, 2020). More recently, passion for work has been theorized by Adam Davidson (2020a), who argues that it will become the key feature of tomorrow's economy – which he calls the Passion Economy. According to Davidson, as Western societies move further and further away from the traditional 9-to-5 model, workers and employers collectively redefine what labour, dedication, and purpose at work mean.[1] The Passion Economy, he argues, combines economic success with the development of each worker's individual talent: this new economy will reward passion, the way the traditional economy rewarded sacrifices. This model is presented as the solution to contemporary work-related ills – the burnouts, the effects of the COVID19 pandemic on work relationship, the great resignation, the quiet quitting, and many others. This chapter analyses Davidson's argument, and the general emphasis on passion for work from a moral standpoint. It seeks to answer the following: What role does passion play for corporations, and does it effectively contribute to workers' wellbeing? Why are workers expected to be passionate? Is passion really the solution to our increasingly difficult relationship with traditional work? Should passion be used as a measurement of success and failures at work?

This chapter starts with the presentation of various work-related ills that seem to affect workers and organizations today and illustrate the ways our collective relationship with work is being reshaped. It then looks at the role that passion is believed to play in attending to these issues, reintroducing meaning in the workplace, and boosting motivation. It presents Davidson's claim that the Passion Economy will replace our traditional understanding of work and that passion will become a key factor of professional success and wellbeing. Without denying that passion for work can be beneficial, we finally argue that Davidson's argument presents significant conceptual and ethical problems. The requirement that passion be an essential feature of a successful work life runs the risk of elitism, but passion also lacks the robustness required to serve as an effective evaluative tool. Finally, we argue that the focus on passion may pose risks to workers' wellbeing: it risks individualizing problems of suffering at work, deterring from looking at collective solutions, and may be used to justify poor treatment of workers, leading to a new type of alienation.

STARTING POINT

In Western societies – and beyond – workers' relationship with their jobs has been going through considerable changes over the past few decades (Kelliher & Richardson, 2019). These changes are multi-faceted: some can be characterized by a sense of hopelessness regarding wage labour, and a desire to conceptually challenge and reshape it – illustrated in its most radical form through the 'anti-work' movement (Lashbrooke, 2021). Others may invite workers to take control over their work life and reject the 'wage slaves' model. For example, we can see in the rise of interest in entrepreneurship (Tuccille, 2021), freelancing (Little, 2022), but also cryptocurrencies a way to either get more flexibility, fight inflation, or increase economic independence (Ellsworth, 2021). What these new forms of work have in common, is the rejection of the traditional 9-to-5 model, which some have called a 'relic of the past' (Kelly, 2021). Phenomena like the great resignation (Kuzior et al., 2022), quiet quitting (Mahand & Caldwell, 2023), or the Chinese concept of 'lying flat' (Zhang & Li, 2023) also indicate a growing disengagement from work and a paradigm shift (Sandro & Fabiola, 2022). This can be explained in numerous ways: more recently, the impact of the COVID19 pandemic, the climate crisis, an increase in work-related health issues such as burnouts, anxiety, or depression, or the rapid introduction of artificial intelligence tools in the workplace may have exacerbated these problems (Ng & Stanton, 2023).

The general feeling seems akin to the disappointment one feels from an unfulfilled promise; in this case, the meritocratic dream that if one works hard enough, one will eventually succeed. This idea is increasingly questioned. Markovits (2019) argues that despite its appearance of fairness, meritocratic competition has become a tool to oppress the middle class and divide society. Sandel (2020) also warns us against the danger of seeing the world through a deserving/undeserving economic and moral dichotomy. Not only is the belief that success will necessarily follow efforts slowly fading, success is also being redefined subjectively – for example, in terms of personal fulfilment rather than financial stability. But what is striking in the critique of conventional labour and movements like the great resignation, is what seems like a common feeling of betrayal, and the shared recognition that hard work did not, in fact, pay off. Many American middle class white-collar workers still struggle to make ends meet, have to face overwhelming student loans, or can only dream of becoming home-owners, and this despite having followed all the meritocratic pathways.

Furthermore, the very concept of the meaning of one's work – or lack thereof – is becoming increasingly relevant and discussed (Pignault & Houssemand, 2021). The phenomenon of 'bullshit jobs', defined by Graeber (2018), illustrates the problem of meaninglessness at work. According to Graeber, 'bullshit jobs' are jobs that, while often scoring high on social status and income, bring little to no value to society or the individuals who have them. Graeber starts with the recognition that the Keynesian promise has remained unfulfilled: Keynes (1930) predicted that technological advancements would lead to a decrease in work hours, at least in countries that benefit the most from such advancements. Keynes has been proven wrong, and the workplace is now facing an asymmetry: on the one hand, technological improvements have indeed decreased the need for workers in multiple domains, while the incentive to work remains stronger than ever – partly due to the lack of financial alternatives. Graeber concludes that this imbalance has led to the creation of a multitude of pointless jobs, in order to serve various superfluous purposes, none of them having any actual utility.

Graeber bluntly writes that 'it's as if someone were out there making up pointless jobs just for the sake of keeping us working' (preface, p. xvi). In the meantime, other essential industries are in great need of workers – public services, healthcare, education, and so on. Graeber explains that despite the apparent facility of their jobs, 'bullshit workers' suffer from the haunting feeling that what they do does not matter for themselves or their community. This leads him to conclude that wellbeing at work is inherently linked to the feeling that what we do somehow contributes in a positive way to society, or at the very least, leads to some sort of self-realization.

But workers don't only want their jobs to be meaningful, they also want to be respected at work. Kong and Belkin (2021) explore the feeling of neglect that some employees have felt from their employers during the COVID19 pandemic. Their study looks at employees who have been asked to make a great deal of sacrifices to keep the economy afloat during the pandemic, but who don't feel that their efforts are reciprocated by their employers. Their findings suggest that a perceived lack of recognition or care from employers significantly impacts how meaningful their jobs appear to be. They argue that feeling neglected at work not only damages employees' perception of their company and jobs, it also affects their personal wellbeing.

The emergence of 'quiet-quitting', another component of the great resignation phenomenon, is often linked to a feeling of asymmetry in the reciprocal relationship that binds workers to their employers (Harter, 2022). Quiet quitting refers to a drop in commitment from the worker to go 'above and beyond' their job duty and a lack of motivation to perform exceptionally well (Formica & Sfodera, 2022). It can be described as a form of disengagement but also as a way to reject 'hustle culture', which glorifies jumping from one meeting to another, working 80 hours a week, or barely having time for lunch. It can also be seen as a way to reclaim the worklife balance that has not been provided, or even as a form of protest by workers who, despite their efforts, fail to see the fruits of their sacrifices. In China, the concept of 'lying-flat' or 'Tang-Ping' (躺平) echoes this idea, but is more related to a form of passive resistant behaviour towards peer competition, especially in the academic context (Hsu, 2022). Started as a social-media trend where school graduates would post photos of themselves lying down while wearing graduation gowns, 'Tang-Ping' expresses a desire to reject the typical 9-9-6 work model (from 9 a.m. to 9 p.m., 6 days a week), and instead pursue hobbies, or simply do nothing at all (Zayaruzny & Hoa, 2023).

The growing numbers of these behaviours and approaches seem to indicate that however we choose to call it, workers are redefining their relationship with work, looking for more meaning, and reclaiming better control over their own lives. Cultivating employees' passion is sometimes seen as a solution to these work-related ills and challenges (Hagel et al., 2014). Boyatzis et al. (2002) suggest reawakening our passion for work, when we 'feel trapped', 'bored', or 'not like the person we want to be' (p. 6). But this proposal, although popular, is not without challenges of its own. The following section will explore the ways passion can and has been utilized by organizations in the hope to increase motivation and performances, as well as the new passion-based economic model conceptualized by

Davidson as the Passion Economy. Later on, the limitations and ethical concerns raised by this use of passion will be examined.

PASSION FOR WORK AND THE PASSION ECONOMY
Definition, History and Benefits

Passion refers to a strong inclination towards an activity, for which passionate agents are willing to dedicate time and energy (Vallerand et al., 2003). It can be divided into two categories: harmonious and obsessive passion: the former refers to an inclination that makes agents autonomously choose what they engage in, while the latter refers to the uncontrolled internalization of the activity, making it coincide with the agent's identity (Vallerand et al., 2003).[2] In the context of work, passion refers to such inclination related to work activities, generating a will to pursue work-related goals (Jung & Sohn, 2022). The interest in passion and its connection with the economy is not new. It is rooted in the long history of organizations' search for legitimate ways to motivate and control employees, but also in reflections on what it means to be a worker, have a meaningful job, or find professional success. Fundamentally, what is at play in these debates is the central questions of how to motivate people to work, boost the economy, and generate as much satisfaction as possible for all parties involved.

Economists and philosophers have tried to answer these questions in a variety of ways. For Adam Smith, market forces are driven by either self-interest, or the need to equilibrate conflicting passions – such as anger, altruism, or loss aversion (Ashraf et al., 2005; Keppler, 2010). In the Marxist tradition, work motivation cannot be separated from class struggle and alienation. Under capitalism, workers are alienated from the product of their labour and therefore deprived of the satisfaction of taking part in the creation process. However, human beings for Marx are not meant to remain passive consumers, but are naturally active producers, capable of self-realizing through labour. A proletarian revolution is therefore needed in order to overcome alienation and reestablish the emancipating value of work (Harvey, 2017; Raekstad, 2018; Sayers, 2005). On a very different end of the spectrum, Milton Friedman (1970) denies that businesses hold any social responsibility, and argues that they should merely focus on profit maximization. From this perspective, workers' wellbeing or passion is a point of interest only insofar as it positively impacts the company.

The neoliberal turn has pushed corporations to look at behavioural theory to understand and make use of the mechanisms behind agents' reactions and motives (Stiegler, 2019). It has been argued that in the 20th century, organizations have tended to shift from a coercive to a rational model of worker's control (Barley & Kunda, 1992), focussing on workers' internal dispositions rather than external incentives. Looking for passionate workers can be a good way to meet two simultaneous goals: increase internal incentives to work and avoid the morally and financially costly use of corporate coercion.

More recently, passion has been advocated as a remedy for the collective work-related crises of the 21st century: it is said to be a way to boost employees' motivation, organizations' performances, and overall wellbeing (Vallerand & Houlfort, 2019). From LinkedIn posts to business ethics research papers, the idea that if one wants to be happy and successful at work, one must be passionate about their job, seems increasingly popular. It can help answer the question of corporation legitimacy: how well organizations cultivate workers' passion can determine their level of respectability and ensure employees' commitment.

For organizations, hiring passionate workers presents certain advantages. From a behaviourist perspective, studying the effects of passion can be a way to understand and predict what attitudes are to be expected from agents (Moeller, 2013), how to motivate them or influence their choices.[3] Passion can also act as a driving force: when compared to passionless activities, passionate ones tend to produce unique outcomes (Leider, 2015). Pradhan et al. (2017, p. 3) write that 'passion encompasses challenge, an element of ease and joy at work that transforms purpose into effective performance'. The key distinction is that passion comes from within: to be passionate about a project is to personally desire a particular outcome, which significantly differs from merely following externally imposed rules. Passion and personal identity are also intertwined (Csikszentmihalyi et al., 1993). passion is directly connected to one's individual interests, personal engagement, and self-accomplishment (Pollack et al., 2020).

Finally, passion can boost creativity, and the desire to gain sufficient knowledge to pursue personal goals (Kunat, 2018). Because of this, it can be presented as a positive moderator between purpose and performance (Pradhan et al., 2017). Unsurprisingly, more and more companies claim to seek to hire passionate individuals, and not simply workers with experience or prestigious diplomas (Polson, 2020; Thiefelds, 2017). Passion creates committed, hard-working, flexible, and innovative employees, whose dedication to their tasks will directly be linked to their own sense of personal achievement and self-realization. Going back to Friedman, companies can regard passion for work as a fruitful investment: if it is shown that passion produces better performances, then it is in a business's interest not only to look for passionate workers but also to create them.

The Passion Economy

But passion is not only a way to transform one's relationship with work or make employees more efficient, it can also be seen as the key concept of a new type of economy. This is what Adam Davidson (2020a) theorizes in his book *The Passion Economy*, in which he describes the increasingly central role that passion plays and will continue to play in reshaping the 21st century. According to Davidson, the traditional vision of work that has dominated the last few decades will be replaced by a passion-based model. Work, he says, need no longer be synonymous with sacrifices and suffering: doing something you truly love can in fact be the key to professional success and wellbeing. Davidson suggests that we challenge the typical dichotomy that opposes sacrificial but financially secure work, to passion-driven but unstable jobs. Using the example of his own father and grandfather, he argues that the generational confrontation between a factory worker and a struggling artist is no longer relevant: in today's economy, we no longer have to make this choice. What it takes, he argues, is a 'shift of perspective', 'hard work', and the recognition that passion and business can and should be interdependent. Davidson considers this model to be the future of work, but so do many in economic or business circles (Amitabh, 2022),[4] including, for example, web3 investor Li Jin, self-identified as 'Passion Economy pioneer' (Li, 2021).

Davidson's claim relies on the premise that we all have a unique passion or talent to explore. Once we have identified what we love to do and do well, we should make it the centre of our business or work life. Davidson predicts that tomorrow's economy will value passion the way the 20th century valued sacrifices and devotion – although passion does not exclude these concepts. The novelty of the Passion Economy consists in its call for self-realization, and the importance of cultivating one's individuality over following rules. While the traditional economy valued standardization and conformity, Davidson argues that the Passion Economy praises individual differences. He asks the following: 'How many people continue in jobs they don't love, working for insufficient wages, because they don't believe they have the inherent gifts necessary to follow their dreams and take control of their economic lives?' (Davidson, 2020a; p. 21). To him, passion is the answer to our collective concerns about work and loss of faith in our ability to find meaning through it.

Davidson also argues that his theory is inclusive, and that the Passion Economy concerns all kinds of sectors, not only start-ups or white-collars positions. He uses the example of a brush-maker, whose declining family business flourished again when the youngest member of the family came out with a unique solution to a specific problem. To Davidson, this illustrates the Passion Economy perfectly: success comes as a result of talent development and narrow problem-fixing – which he calls 'pursuing intimacy at scale' (Davidson, 2020a; p. 101). This is also meant to demonstrate the inclusivity of this new framework: brush-makers, but also accountants or wine producers, all can partake in this new economy.

There are however some rules that one must follow: Davidson identifies eight of them, which are meant to guarantee professional success in this new economic framework. They range from 'only create value that can't be easily copied' (p. 49), to 'passion is a story' (p. 57) or 'never be in the commodity business, even if you sell what other people consider a commodity' (p. 62). Davidson claims that the Passion Economy is inherently distinct from commodity-selling, although commodification is a trap that one can easily fall into. The difference, he says, lies in that passion businesses sell a unique product, with a unique value and at a unique price – for example, an experience in a nice coffee shop rather than just a coffee. He draws a parallel with workers themselves, arguing that employees in the 20th century were essentially and for the most part seen as commodities. The Passion Economy aims at nurturing each worker's worth by cultivating their unique capabilities, eventually generating profit by the same token. This concept echoes the idea of monetizing life – often found in the content-creator industry (Friedman, 2022). The Passion Economy advocates for a loss of distinction between work life and private life, and opens up the possibility that a personal interest may become a source of revenue. Since passion is meant to boost voluntary decision-making and creativity rather than constraint and order-following, the hope seems to be that this will result in a wellbeing increase for everyone involved.

The rise of entrepreneurship can be seen as the illustration of the increasing importance people place on passion as a significant motivation for their career goals (Thorgren et al., 2014). Entrepreneurship is an economic driver that impacts growth and a sector that continues to attract workers (Li et al., 2020). Unsurprisingly, passion is often an essential aspect of entrepreneurship, as it has a significant impact on entrepreneurial behaviour (Cardon et al., 2013; Santos & Cardon, 2019). All of this suggests that passion could in appearance become a key concept in today's and tomorrow's economy. Despite its popularity, the Passion Economy as described by Davidson presents various limitations. Furthermore, passion as a work requirement raises significant moral concerns that the following section will explore.

THE ETHICS OF PASSION AT WORK

The idea that there could be anything worrying about the Passion Economy is not self-evident. In fact, Davidson's claim relies on two seemingly true premises: first, our relationship with the workplace and our definition of ourselves as workers are changing. Second, it is desirable that workers question the legitimacy of the rules they are under, and seek for more meaning in the workplace. This shift of perspective seems unavoidable, at least for a significant portion of the working population in Western societies. One may therefore wonder what could be so wrong in shifting from sacrifices to passion. Additionally, the problems that workers are pointing out are crucial to address – absence of living wages, necessity to work multiple jobs, alienating 9-to-5 life, and so on. Why not address them by shifting towards a passion-driven economy where people would be free to make profit on what makes them unique and what they love to do? What could possibly be wrong with the Passion Economy?

Despite its promises, passion for work presents significant challenges and limitations that need to be addressed. In this section, we raise three main objections to the idea that fostering passion is the solution to our work-related ills. First, we argue that the focus on passion as a necessary component of professional wellbeing runs the risk of elitism. Second, we argue that passion lacks the conceptual robustness to be a fair and objective measure of work-related success. Finally, we raise further ethical concerns about the potential harm that an over-emphasis on passion could do to workers.

Elitism Objection

In his book, Davidson focusses on what individuals can obtain in the Passion Economy, arguing that all sectors can benefit from it. He writes that 'with a handful of easy-to-learn rules, a shift of perspective, and a bit of hard work, a meaningful marriage of passion and business can be forged, and far more people can do a whole lot better' (Davidson, 2020a, p. 17). Furthermore, Davidson claims that 'to succeed financially we must embrace our unique passions" (p. 15), positioning passion as a necessary condition for success. But is the Passion Economy as accessible as Davidson believes, and can anyone really be passionate about their job?

Davidson's descriptions seem to start from a position where individuals already meet the conditions for passion-driven careers. Even assuming that everyone possesses a specific talent to develop, many conditions need to be met before it can be turned into a career – for example, education, financial stability, time, network, and energy, to name a few. Davidson never mentions these prerequisites, neither does he suggest how they could be pursued. Access to the Passion Economy seems restricted to those who already meet the necessary conditions for it, which often indicates a certain privilege (Cappelle, 2022). This is actually something that Davidson admits himself in an interview for World Affairs, seemingly contradicting his claim that 'it is up to us to find our own path, to define, uniquely for ourselves, what we want and what we have to offer' (Davidson, 2020b, p. 262). Asked how this new model can be made accessible, Davidson answers that although very few of the actors he mentions in his book were born wealthy, some sort of safety net seems necessary: 'If you're living paycheque to paycheque (…) I don't think it's realistic that you're gonna be able to take risks' (Davidson, 2020b). He concedes that some amount of privileges might be helpful, if not necessary, to flourish in this economy. Unfortunately, Davidson does not provide any instruction on how to reach social mobility in this new model.

Furthermore, the Passion Economy continues to follow a meritocratic path, and in doing so, does not significantly differ from a more traditional economy. The meritocratic ideal is based on the normative belief that personal merit – whether that is effort or talent – should be the measure of distributive justice (Mulligan, 2018). This view can be criticized on a number of fronts; more particularly, it has been argued that the meritocratic proposal is deeply elitist, as it remains blind to the social and economic hindrances to mobility and professional success (Mijs & Savage, 2020). Similarly, the ability to develop a passion, or even have a talent for something, either may not be shared by everyone, or may only be accessible assuming that some conditions are met. The claim that success in the Passion Economy only takes a paradigm shift and some hard work seems unrealistic, and blind to the arbitrary nature of what impacts people's careers.

The non-inclusivity of the Passion Economy raises further ethical questions related to equity and justice: if we claim that the economy of the 21st century relies on passion jobs, what are we to do about careers that have nothing to do with passion? If we consider passion to be a necessary condition for happiness at work and financial success, we necessarily leave out jobs that fail to meet such condition. However, it is conceivable that some jobs may never inspire passion and may never be part of the Passion Economy. This does not mean that these jobs cannot be meaningful. Blue-collar manual jobs, for example, are valuable not only for society but often also for the workers themselves, despite the commonly shared assumption that these jobs lack intrinsic value besides the paycheque (Saari et al., 2022). This could also be said about any low-skill jobs, 'pink-collar', jobs of the care industry, or 'grunt' work (Chen, 2020), characterized by its dullness and lack of social prestige. Despite their lack of financial and social recognition, these jobs provide immense value to society, as it has been particularly highlighted during the COVID19 pandemic. Yet, while many workers can feel passionate about these jobs, it is not self-evident that they all do, or that passion is even relevant at all in these cases. Meaning, satisfaction over a job well done, and passion are very different things. It is conceivable that no worker is intrinsically passionate about collecting waste, cleaning public toilets, or work at a fast-food chain restaurant. But this should not determine their level of wellbeing, financial stability, or social recognition.

To say that the economy of the future will value and be centred around passion runs the risk of excluding potentially 'passionless' industries and workers. That is not to say that passion-driven careers are unimportant, but rather that the move towards a new economy should include those who are in the most vulnerable social and economic position before improving the life of an already privileged few. Finally, the elitism of this concept can be demonstrated using Rawls' two principles of justice, which demand equal opportunity of access to offices and positions, and claim that social inequalities can only be justified when they benefit the most disadvantaged members of society – also known as the difference principle (Rawls, 1999). The Passion Economy as presented by Davidson fails to meet both conditions: first, as it is designed for workers who already benefit from either social economic advantages, or safety nets, it fails to meet the condition of equal access opportunity. Second, as it leaves behind passionless careers and industries, it violates the difference principle. According to Rawls (1985) and the principles of justice as fairness, social rules that fail to satisfy these two principles of justice are unfair, and so would be the Passion Economy as presented here.

Although being passionate about our jobs is probably desirable, passion should not be a requirement, nor should it be relevant when it comes to determine financial success or professional wellbeing. The Passion Economy only focusses on the internal conditions individuals must meet to enter this economy (work, talent, dedication, etc.), but never mentions external social or economic factors. It runs the risk of unfairness, as it seems designed for certain industries only, and has very little to propose regarding the most vulnerable portions of the economy.

Relevance and Robustness Objection

The Passion Economy seems to rely on the assumption that people all have either a talent to develop or a passion to pursue. Davidson (2020a) insists on the 'unique value' that passion-businesses bring compared to other, more generic ones (p. 62). He however never quite contemplates the possibility that some workers, while being unique individuals, might simply not have a unique business idea or product to propose to the market. In fact, many workers might only ever have average skills or talents that they share with millions of others, while remaining perfectly competent at what they do. Plenty might not have a passion at all.

Additionally, passion is not necessarily something individuals are aware of as they start their professional life, but it can be discovered along the way. In this case, the discovery and pursuit of a passion could be facilitated by the appropriate conditions, which Davidson never really mentions (e.g. time, peer-support, flexibility, etc.). It is also possible that rather than searching for our individual talents, humans produce better results when they collaborate and gather their competences. In many situations, skill-uniqueness and individuality might be less relevant or fruitful than collaboration. The Passion Economy focusses a lot on what individuals bring to the table, but little on the value of cooperation and collectiveness in the workplace. However, it has been shown that collaboration in the workplace can increase intrinsic motivation, task persistence, and overall enjoyment (Carr & Walton, 2014). Collective intelligence, which is the ability of a group to arrive at solutions that individual group members would fail to find alone, has been proven to increase innovation in enterprises (Lee & Jin, 2019). Although the Passion Economy does not exclude collaboration, its insistence on unique individual passion runs the risk of overlooking the social and collective nature of the workplace, as well as the possibility that better results might be produced with the help of others.

All of this seems to indicate that passion might not be as relevant as Davidson claims, even for white-collar professions. The premise that everyone has a particular talent seems overly optimistic at best, guilty of wishing-thinking at worst. Moreover, the focus placed on passion seems to undermine how important other factors of work success and wellbeing could be: collaboration, work conditions, room for self and collective discovery, time, and many others.

But passion for work does not only lack relevance, it also lacks robustness. Passion is highly personal, and difficult to measure in a way that could reliably be used in all work sectors (Chen et al., 2020). The objects of my passions are also personal, and my passionate feelings might never be transferable to others, irrespective of their strength. Because of this, passion can only be evaluated in subjective terms. The intensity, duration, reasons for my passion for something are properties that only I can describe. Passion can also come and go overtime. The interpretation of what talent means also seems to vary greatly from person to person, and finding a single definition has been proven challenging (Gallardo-Gallardo, 2018).

A new economic model, however, must meet certain objective conditions: organizations should be able to measure work performances in a robust and reliable way. Using passion as an evaluative tool, or as a condition for success, seems at odds with the demands of fairness and stability that a workplace should meet. This is especially important as these conditions will have a direct and concrete impact on people's professional and financial lives. The terms that we use to make such evaluations should therefore be clearly defined, intelligible, and easily measurable – for workers and organizations. Passion, on the other hand, is often defined broadly and ambiguously. Most importantly, its inherent subjectivity makes it vulnerable to misinterpretation and misevaluation. It essentially lacks the conceptual robustness to provide a normative measure of who will win the economic game.

The elitist objection, coupled with concerns regarding relevance and robustness, should alert us to the following: who gets to partake in 'the future of work', and who does not? The requirement of passion necessarily excludes a significant portion of workers – largely blue, but also pink-collar workers – raising concerns about how power is distributed in the workplace. Ultimately, it is tempting to see illustrated through this model yet another – perhaps more glamourous – version of class antagonism (Marx, 1848): the long-lasting competition between those who have the means to be passionate decision-makers and those who are simply executors.

The Risks of Passion

After examining who is excluded from the Passion Economy – namely, a large portion of the working class – this section explores the ill-effects of passion for jobs in which it is either encouraged or required. The Passion Economy is not only conceptually problematic; the insistence on passion as an essential component of a successful work life can also cause harm. Davidson (2020a) argues that small business owners who follow the passion model have reported to be 'richer, happier, and more deeply fulfilled' (p. 84). The popular expression 'choose a job you love and you will never have to work a day in your life'[5] illustrates the commonly shared belief that as long as we love our work, it will not feel like a burden. The hope is that workers will feel intimately connected to their jobs, and as a result, will be more motivated, freer, and happier. But although passion jobs can be rewarding for those who have them, they can also pose significant problems for personal freedom and wellbeing.

We have seen that passion can be divided into two categories: harmonious and obsessive (Vallerand et al., 2003). It has been shown that harmonious passion for work can improve life satisfaction and contribute to workers' happiness (Yukhymenko-Lescroart & Sharma, 2022). But, on the other hand, obsessive passion for work can produce the opposite effect: it can make workers feel pressure to perform a certain way, increase demands, and generally negatively affect their relationship with their workplace (Cabrita & Duarte, 2023). Obsessive passion can lead to compulsively pursuing or struggling to cease the activity in question, leading to a loss of self-control, and possibly an increase in feelings of shame, guilt, and stress (Morales, 2020). Vallerand et al. (2010) argue that obsessive passion for work can create conflicts between work duties and other life activities, and that this conflict contributes to burnout. In the case, where passion is a component of the job, it is important that organizations facilitate harmonious passion, and make sure obsessive passion does not take over. However, the Passion Economy as described by Davidson, does not explain how to cultivate harmonious passion only, nor does it mention the possibility of harm caused by obsessive passion. In fact, harmonious passion requires various work conditions: managers' leadership style, a supportive environment, or a sense of belongingness can all positively impact employees' harmonious sense of passion (Spehar et al., 2016). What this seems to suggest, is that passion has a lot to do with social environment and work conditions, and can therefore be cultivated rather than expected as a prerequisite.

However, we can also question whether harmonious passion is always conducive to more wellbeing. Even in the case of harmonious passion for work, the line between work duties and personal life should be clearly defined. When that is not the case – for example, in freelancing or entrepreneurial jobs – workers can experience stress and alienation just as much as traditional 9-to-5 employees (Kaur, 2019). Workers may have a harmoniously passionate relationship with their work, but still remain under significant pressure, if their work duties become too demanding, and leave no time or energy for other activities. Teaching is often considered to be a passion-driven career (Rampa, 2012). However, teachers can also experience stress, anxiety, and burnouts due to increasing workload and pressure imposed by neoliberal educational and managerial systems (Mahmoodi-Shahrebabaki, 2019). This suggests that wellbeing at work is not separable from external conditions, and that passion, however harmonious, cannot always make up for a lack of support, a stressful environment, or an overly demanding workload. Although passion is not what directly causes the harm, problems happen when it is expected to compensate for poor work conditions, or used to increase work hours.[6] Harmonious passion for work might be beneficial in most cases, but it should never be used as an excuse to neglect other essential factors of wellbeing at work. Passion workers can also have other passions: to have a passion job does not mean being willing to sacrifice time dedicated to other activities. As rewarding a job can be, if it takes all workers' time and energy, they can still suffer from pressure, or have to neglect other activities they deem worthy of pursuit. In other words, passion may cause harm if used as the only measure of workers' satisfaction, if it leads to neglecting one's health and wellbeing, or if it deters companies from paying attention to material work conditions.

From the workers' perspective, the assumption that passion jobs lead to more freedom can also be questioned. Assuming that one's passion is their favourite activity, it could be tempting to assume that passionate workers benefit from more freedom than people forced to work on something that they haven't chosen or dislike. But this would be a limited view of what freedom is, or could be. Hobbes (1994) defined freedom as non-frustration to preferred option: if an agent prefers option A to option B, and if option A only is available, then the agent's freedom while picking A is perfectly intact. On the other hand, if option A is unavailable, according to Hobbes their choice is frustrated, the agent is therefore unfree. This view carries significant problems and inherent contradictions – for example, the fact that I can simply choose to become free by adapting my preference to available options (Pettit, 2011). Freedom cannot be defined by the possibility to pick a preferred option only, but rather should be understood as the expansion of available options, the expansion being as large as legally, morally, or socially possible. If a passion job takes so much time that it makes all other possibilities unavailable, then passion workers are no freer than others: the fact that they work on their favourite activity does not make up for their lack of options.

There are reasons to fear that the Passion Economy might simply be another form of 'hustle culture'. The difference being that jumping from one meeting to another, skipping lunch break, or working overtime would be justified by passion rather than coercion. But fundamentally, effects on workers would be roughly the same. Furthermore, focusing on passion could make these ills even harder for workers to identify and complain about; after all, who would not want to dedicate all they can to their passion? Work takes on a misplaced moral dimension: a lack of success becomes a moral failure to show enough commitment or love for the job. The focus on passion individualizes work-related issues. Instead of looking at how to improve structures, environments, or conditions, the Passion Economy allows us to blame individual workers for their lack of success – or passion. This could generate guilt, a sense of personal failure, or increase self-imposed demands to an unhealthy level (Loriol & Leroux, 2015).

Passion can be a problem if it becomes yet another work-related injunction, another goal to reach, and another key performance indicator. We have no reason to consider that passion eliminates the possibility of exploitation or commodification of workers: in fact, it could increase it. Kim et al. (2020) argue that the emphasis on passion can mask a modern form of exploitation, and be used to legitimize poor treatment of workers. According to them, this legitimization is illustrated through the assumption that passionate workers would volunteer for the job, if given the opportunity, and that the passion job is a reward in itself. This idea seems to echo Legge's (1999) view on organizations' treatment of employees. She argues that businesses tend to see employees as non-human commodities or resources, but choose to use humanizing ways to describe them, such as 'team' or 'family' members.[7] However, she claims, even these terms call into question workers' autonomy: a family member is intrinsically and emotionally linked to other members, and it is unclear how free they are to detach from them – in fact, detaching from them would often be seen as a moral failure. An interesting parallel can be drawn with passion: a seemingly inspirational concept can be a cover for unreasonable demands and objectification of passionate workers. Failure to perform becomes failure to sufficiently care, which calls into question people's personal values, sense of duty, and loyalty.

Passion workers are no less human capital than other workers if work conditions are neglected. Foucault (1978–1979) describes *homo economicus* as 'an entrepreneur, an entrepreneur of himself'. Neoliberal market, for him, is characterized by the fact that everyone can see themselves as an entrepreneur, which carries not only economic but also political consequences, and leads to the creation of a new form of subjectivity (Read, 2009). We can draw a parallel between this idea and Davidson's claim that the Passion Economy is for everyone – although we have seen that it is not. Is the passion worker simply a new *homo economicus*? Can passionate workers also suffer from alienation? Alienation can be defined as the impossibility for workers to have control over their own activity and the product of their labour (Cukier, 2017). But as capital is becoming more and more personified, workers as *homo economicus* become at the same time the source of their revenue and 'the author of their own satisfaction' (Candiotto, 2017; Foucault, 1978–1979, p. 232). Unfortunately, this new relationship between the subject and its labour does not exclude new forms of alienation as well. Alienation, for the *homo economicus*, could precisely come from the indistinguishableness between the subject and the product of her work, or from the intensity of the emotions workers feel about their tasks – whether it is deep care for a project, guilt about not doing enough, anxiety that the project will not work, etc. Trott (2017) suggests that the emotional intensity of the working day carries the same consequences for workers as its length. While for Marx (1867), the length and physical demands of the work days contribute to alienation – and therefore emotional detachment – today the expectation that one deeply cares about their work might produce a similar exhaustion. Having to be constantly engaged can create a moral fatigue and a new form of alienation, that here is not characterized by a lack of control but precisely by the expectation that workers are constantly in control. Furthermore, by individualizing work outcomes, passion can alienate workers from others – as they are personally blamed for their failures, or praised for their achievements.

The Passion Economy gives us the opportunity to redefine what it means for workers to be commodified, alienated, or exploited, in an economy where their success or failure is often attributed to their individual effort, passion, or lack thereof. More research needs to be done on the precise forms that these ills might take, and on how to build an economy that addresses rather than creates them.

CONCLUSION

In this chapter, we have shown that passion often appears to be a solution for the collective ills that many workers are experiencing, as well as a way to reintroduce meaning in the workplace. It is increasingly sought by companies as it can improve motivation, be considered a reward in itself, or lead to better results. The Passion Economy illustrates these views, and many predict it to be the future of work. However, we have argued that the requirement that workers be passionate about their jobs, or the assumption that a lack of passion is the reason for their work-related problems, is elitist and fails to address the real causes of a lack of wellbeing at work. Furthermore, passion lacks conceptual robustness to serve as an adequate measure of distributive justice, in the workplace and beyond. Finally, we saw that the requirement of passion for work can cause harm to workers, even in professions where passion is a key element. It can be used to justify exploitation, neglect work conditions, and may create a new form of alienation that comes from the expectation to always be emotionally and personally engaged with our tasks, to the point of saturation. Passion does not provide a satisfactory model to redefine our economy; in fact, the Passion Economy does not significantly differ from the capitalist and neoliberal systems that have dominated most of the organizational world since the 19th and early 20th centuries. Of course, passion at work is not in itself a problem: in fact, loving a job is often a privilege and something many workers look for. Issues emerge when passion becomes another work duty. We know that improving work conditions and social support have positive effects on workers (Loscocco & Spitze, 1990). At the end of the day, it is unclear whether passion is really an attainable goal for all, but it is clear that most workers could benefit from living wages, good insurance policies, sufficient paid holidays, or stable retirement plans. Before switching to a new economy that does not address these factors, the priority should be on fixing material problems that have been proven to significantly and sustainably benefit all workers. Instead of individualizing work problems, the importance of looking for collective solutions seems more important than ever. Much work needs to be done on how to (re)introduce meaning at work, and move towards an economic model that is inclusive, equitable, and sustainable. Focussing on external work conditions and social environments seems to be a good start. But workers could also be given more control over their own conditions, through more internal deliberation and collaboration, more checks and balances, or more horizontal structures. Passion need not be a prerequisite, but it can be an end goal: something workers should have the possibility to cultivate, whether it is at work or outside of work, alone or with others. The possibility of passion could be understood as a side-effect of a healthy work life, and a sign that organizations are effectively working towards workers' emancipation.

NOTES

1. See, for example, Cappelle (2022).
2. The implications of harmonious and obsessive passion for work are further discussed in The Risks of Passion section.
3. See, for example, Thaler and Sunstein (2008), on how companies and lawmakers can use choice-architecture techniques to obtain a certain outcome from the public or customers.
4. See also Author Unknown (2022).
5. It is unclear where this quote originally comes from. See https://quoteinvestigator.com/2014/09/02/job-love/ for some hypothesis.
6. See, for example, Indeed Editorial Team (2022).
7. On the concerns with calling a workplace a family, see Luna (2021).

REFERENCES

Amitabh, U. (2022). *How the passion economy is shaping the future of work*. World Economic Forum.
Ashraf, A., Camerer, C. F., & Loewenstein, G. (2005). Adam Smith, behavioral economist. *Journal of Economic Perspectives, 19*(3), 131–145.
Author Unknown. (2014, September 2). Choose a job you love and you will never have to work a day in your life. Quote Investigator. https://quoteinvestigator.com/2014/09/02/job-love/
Author Unknown. (2022). Passion economy: What it is and why it is the future of work. Passion.io. https://passion.io/blog/passion-economy-future-of-work
Barley, S. R., & Kunda, G. (1992). Design and devotion: Surges of rational and normative ideologies of control in managerial discourse. *Administrative Science Quarterly, 37*(3), 363–399. https://doi.org/10.2307/2393449
Boyatzis, R., McKee, A., & Goleman, D. (2002). Reawakening your passion for work. *Harvard Business Review*. Retrieved from https://hbr.org/2002/04/reawakening-your-passion-for-work.
Cabrita, C., & Duarte, A. P. (2023). Passionately demanding: Work passion's role in the relationship between work demands and affective well-being at work. *Frontiers in Psychology, 14*, 1053455. https://doi.org/10.3389/fpsyg.2023.1053455
Candiotto, C. (2017). Le néolibéralisme américain et l'ambigüité de l'*homo oeconomicus* chez Michel Foucault. *Cahiers critiques de philosophie, 18*, 93–108. https://doi.org/10.3917/ccp.018.0093.
Cappelle, A. (2022). *The passion economy is pure nonsense*. YouTube. https://www.youtube.com/watch?v=2wVqXW_18NY&t=447s
Cardon, M. S., Gregoire, D. A., Stevens, C. E., & Patel, P. C. (2013). Measuring entrepreneurial passion: Conceptual foundations and scale validation. *Journal of Business Venturing, 28*, 373–396. https://doi.org/10.1016/j.jbusvent.2012.03.003
Carr, P. B., & Walton, G. M. (2014). Cues of working together fuel intrinsic motivation. *Journal of Experimental Social Psychology, 53*, 169–184.

Chen, J. (2020, July 12). *Grunt work*. Investopedia. https://www.investopedia.com/terms/g/grunt-work.asp

Chen, P., Lee, F., & Lim, S. (2020). Loving thy work: developing a measure of work passion. *European Journal of Work and Organizational Psychology*, 29(1), 140–158. https://doi.org/10.1080/1359432X.2019.1703680

Csikszentmihalyi, M., Rathunde, K., & Whalen, S. (1993). *Talented teenagers: The roots of success and failure*. Cambridge.

Cukier, A. (2017). Entrepreneur de soi ou travailleur aliéné? Penser l'organisation néomanagériale du travail avec et au-delà de Foucault. *Néolibéralisme et subjectivité*, 6. https://doi.org/10.4000/teth.918

Davidson, A. (2020a). *The passion economy, the new rules for thriving in the twenty-first century*. Alfred A. Knopf.

Davidson, A. (2020b, January 21). *The new rules of 21st century passion economy* [Interview for World Affairs (with Jessie Wisdom. Moderator: Markos Kounalakis)]. YouTube. https://www.worldaffairs.org/event-calendar/event/2020

Ellsworth, B. (2021, June 22). As Venezuela's economy regresses, crypto fills the gaps. *Reuters*. https://www.reuters.com/technology/venezuelas-economy-regresses-crypto-fills-gaps-2021-06-22/

Formica, S., & Sfodera, F. (2022). The great resignation and quiet quitting paradigm shifts: An overview of current situation and future research directions. *Journal of Hospitality Marketing & Management*, 31(8), 899–907. https://doi.org/10.1080/19368623.2022.2136601.

Foucault, M. (1978–1979). *Naissance de la Biolopotique: Cours au Collège de France*. Hautes Etudes.

Friedman, M. (1970) The social responsibility of business is to increase its profits. *New York Times Magazine*, 13 September, pp. 122–126.

Friedman, N. (2022, June 13). *The monetized life*. Medium. https://wordworking.medium.com/the-monetized-life-d95f6f2a3b31

Gallardo-Gallardo, E. (2018). The meaning of talent in the world of work. In D. G. Collings, H. Scullion, & P. M. Caligiuri (Eds.), *Global talent management*. Routledge.

Graeber, D. (2018). *Bullshit jobs: A theory*. Simon & Schuster.

Hagel, J., Brown, J. S., Ranjan, A., & Byler, D. (2014). *Passion at work: Cultivating worker passion as a cornerstone of talent developments* [Report from the Deloitte Center for the Edge]. Deloitte University Press.

Harter, J. (2022, September 6). *Is quiet quitting real?*. Gallup. https://www.gallup.com/workplace/398306/quiet-quitting-real.aspx

Harvey, D. (2017). *Marx, capital, and the madness of economic reason*. Profile Books Ltd.

Hobbes, T. (1994). Leviathan. In E. Curley (Ed.), *Leviathan*, with Selected Variants from the Latin Edition of 1668. Hackett.

Hsu, H. Y. (2022). How do Chinese people evaluate "Tang-Ping" (lying flat) and effort-making: The moderation effect of return expectation. *Frontiers in Psychology*, 13, 871439.

Indeed Editorial Team. (2022, October 7). *A concise guide on the importance of passion for work*. Indeed. https://in.indeed.com/career-advice/career-development/importance-of-passion-for-work

Jung, Y., & Sohn, Y. W. (2022). Does work passion benefit or hinder employee's career commitment? The mediating role of work–family interface and the moderating role of autonomy support. *PLoS ONE*, 17(6), e0269298. https://doi.org/10.1371/journal.pone.0269298

Kaur, D. (2019, September 4). *Freelancer burn-out is real. Here's how you can avoid it*. Freelancermap. https://www.freelancermap.com/blog/freelancer-burnout/

Kelliher, C., & Richardson, J. (2019). *Work, working and work relationships in a changing world*. Routledge.

Kelly, J. (2021, July). Working 9-to-5 is and antiquated relic of the past and should be stopped right now. *Forbes*. https://www.forbes.com/sites/jackkelly/2021/07/25/working-9-to-5-is-an-antiquated-relic-from-the-past-and-should-be-stopped-right-now/?sh=4c5e858e40de

Kim, J. Y., Campbell, T. H., Shepherd, S., & Kay, A. C. (2020). Understanding contemporary forms of exploitation: Attributions of passion serve to legitimize the poor treatment of workers. *Journal of Personality and Social Psychology*, 118(1), 121–148. https://doi.org/10.1037/pspi0000190

Keppler, J. H. (2010). *Adam Smith and the economy of the passions* (Routledge Studies in the History of Economics). Routledge.

Keynes, J. M. (1930). Economic possibilities for our grandchildren. In *Essays in persuasion* (pp. 358–373). W.W. Norton & Co. (1963).
Kong, D. T., & Belkin, L. Y. (2021). You don't care for me, so what's the point for me to care for your business? Negative implications of felt neglect by the employer for employee work meaning and citizenship behaviors amid the COVID-19 pandemic. *Journal of Business Ethics. 181*, 645–660.
Kunat, B. (2018). Passion and creativity – Together or separately? *Creativity Theories – Research – Applications, 5*(1), 55–71.
Kuzior, A., Karolina, K., & Łukasz, R. (2022). Great resignation—Ethical, cultural, relational, and personal dimensions of Generation Y and Z employees' engagement. *Sustainability, 14,* (11), 6764. https://doi.org/10.3390/su14116764
Lashbrooke, B. (2021, October 25). The anti-work movement is a sign something's rotten in the workplace. *Forbes.* https://www.forbes.com/sites/barnabylashbrooke/2021/10/25/the-anti-work-movement-is-a-sign-somethings-rotten-in-the-workplace/?sh=38ce34d430ed
Lavigne, G. L., Forest, J., Fernet, C., & Crevier-Braud, L. (2014). Passion at work and workers' evaluations of job demands and resources: A longitudinal study. *Journal of Applied Social Psychology, 44*(4), 255–265. https://doi.org/10.1111/jasp.12209
Lee, J. Y., & Jin, C. H. (2019). How collective intelligence fosters incremental innovation. *Journal of Open Innovation: Technology, Market, and Complexity, 5*(3), 53. https://doi.org/10.3390/joitmc5030053
Legge, K. (1999). Representing people at work. *Organization, 6*(2), 247–264. https://doi.org/10.1177/135050849962005
Leider, R. J. (2015). *The power of purpose-find meaning, live longer, better.* Berret-Koehler Publishers.
Li, C., Murad, M., Shahzad, F., Kham, M. A. S., Ashraf, S. F., & Dogbe, C. S. K. (2020). Entrepreneurial passion to entrepreneurial behavior: Role of entrepreneurial alertness, entrepreneurial self-efficacy and proactive personality. *Frontiers in Psychology, 11,* 1611.
Li, J. (2021). *About me.* https://li-jin.co/about/
Little, B. (2022, January 18). *The growing popularity of freelance work.* Wework https://www.wework.com/ideas/research-insights/research-studies/the-growing-popularity-of-freelance-work.
Loriol, M., & Leroux, N. (2015). *Le travail passionné: l'engagement artistique, sportif ou politique.* Eres.
Loscocco, K. A., & Spitze, G. (1990). Working conditions, social support, and the well-being of female and male factory workers. *Journal of Health and Social Behavior, 31*(4), 313–327.
Luna, J. A. (2021). The toxic effects of branding your workplace a family. *Harvard Business Review.* https://hbr.org/2021/10/the-toxic-effects-of-branding-your-workplace-a-family
Mahand, T., & Caldwell, C. (2023). Quiet quitting: Causes and opportunities. *Business and Management Research, 12*(1), 9–19. https://doi.org/10.5430/bmr.v12n1p9
Mahmoodi-Shahrebabaki, M. (2019). Teacher burnout. In J. I. Liontas (Ed.), *The TESOL encyclopedia of English language teaching* (1–8). John Wiley & Sons.
Markovits, D. (2019). *The meritocracy trap, how America's foundational myth feeds inequality, dismantles the middle class, and devours the elite.* Penguin Press.
Marx, K. (1848). Manifesto of the Communist Party. https://www.marxists.org/archive/marx/works/1848/communist-manifesto/ch01.htm
Marx, K. (1867). Chapter 10: The working day. In Das kapital. https://www.marxists.org/archive/marx/works/1867-c1/ch10.htm#S1
Mijs, J. J. B., & Savage, M. (2020). Meritocracy, elitism and inequality. *The Political Quarterly, 91,* 397–404. https://doi.org/10.1111/1467-923X.12828.
Moeller, J. (2013). Passion as concept of the psychology of motivation. Conceptualization, assessment, inter-individual variability and long-term stability [Ph.D. thesis, University of Erfurt].
Morales, J. (2020, August 8). Two types of passion: Harmonious versus obsessive. *Psychology Today.* https://www.psychologytoday.com/us/blog/building-the-habit-hero/202008/two-types-passion-harmonious-vs-obsessive
Mulligan, T. (2018). *Justice and the meritocratic state.* Routledge.
Ng, E., & Stanton, P. (2023). Editorial: The great resignation: managing people in a post COVID-19 pandemic world. *Personnel Review, 52*(2), 401–407. https://doi.org/10.1108/PR-03-2023-914
Pettit, P. (2011). The instability of freedom as noninterference: The case of Isaiah Berlin. *Ethics, 121*(4), 693–716.

Pignault, A., & Houssemand, C. (2021). What factors contribute to the meaning of work? A validation of Morin's meaning of work questionnaire. *Psicologia, reflexao e critica: revista semestral do Departamento de Psicologia da UFRGS, 34*(1), 2. https://doi.org/10.1186/s41155-020-00167-4

Pollack, J. M., Ho, V. T., O'Boyle E. H., & Kirkman B. L. (2020). Passion at work: A meta-analysis of individual work outcomes. *Journal of Organizational Behavior, 41*(3), 1–21.

Polson, B. (2020, March 10). Four ways to hire passionate employees who actually want to work for you. *Forbes*. https://www.forbes.com/sites/forbescoachescouncil/2020/03/10/four-ways-to-hire-passionate-employees-who-actually-want-to-work-for-you/?sh=2d41da3c21e7

Pradhan, R. K., Panda, P., & Jena, L. K. (2017, October 12). Purpose, passion, and performance at the workplace: Exploring the nature, structure, and relationship. *The Psychologist-Manager Journal, 20*(4), 222–245. Advance online publication. http://dx.doi.org/10.1037/mgr0000059

Raekstad, P. (2018). Human development and alienation in the thought of Karl Marx. *European Journal of Political Theory, 17*(3), 300–323.

Rampa, S. H. (2012). Passion for teaching: A qualitative study. *Procedia: Social and Behavioral Sciences, 47*, 1281–1285.

Rawls, J. (1985). Justice as fairness: Political not metaphysical. *Philosophy and Public Affairs, 14*(3), 223–251.

Rawls, J. (1999). *A theory of justice* (2nd ed.). Harvard University Press.

Read, J. (2009). A genealogy of homo economicus: neoliberalism and the production of subjectivity. *Foucault Studies, 6*, 25–36.

Saari, T., Leinonen, M., & Tapanila, K. (2022). Sources of meaningful work for blue-collar workers. *Social Sciences, 11*(1), 2. https://doi.org/10.3390/socsci11010002

Sandel, M. (2020). *The tyranny of merit: What's become of the common good?* Farrar, Straus and Giroux.

Sandro, F., & Fabiola, S. (2022). The great resignation and quiet quitting paradigm shifts: An overview of current situation and future research directions. *Journal of Hospitality Marketing & Management, 31*(8), 899–907.

Santos, S. C., & Cardon, M. S. (2019). What's love got to do with it? Team entrepreneurial passion and performance in new venture teams. *Entrepreneurship Theory and Practice, 43*, 475–504. https://doi.org/10.1177/1042258718812185

Sayers, S. (2005). Why work? Marx and human nature. *Science & Society, 69*(4), 606–616.

Spehar, I., Forest, J., & Stenseng, F. (2016). Passion for work, job satisfaction, and the mediating role of belongingness. *Scandinavian Journal of Organizational Psychology, 8*(1), 17–26.

Stiegler, B. (2019). *"Il faut s'adapter": sur un nouvel impératif politique*. Gallimard.

Thaler, R. H., & Sunstein, C. R. (2008). *Nudge: Improving decisions about health, wealth, and happiness*. Penguin.

Thiefelds, J. (2017). *The importance of hiring a passionate tribe for your startup*. Company Culture– Hire. https://hire.trakstar.com/blog/importance-hiring-passionate-tribe-startup#:~:text=The%20importance%20of%20hiring%20passionate%20employees&text=Here's%20why%3A,what%20the%20company%20is%20doing

Thorgren, S., Nordström, C., & Wincent, J. (2014). Hybrid entrepreneurship: The importance of passion. *Baltic Journal of Management, 9*(3), 314–329. https://doi.org/10.1108/BJM-11-2013-0175

Trott, B. (2017). Affective labour and alienation: Spinoza's materialism and the sad passions of post-Fordist work. *Emotion, Space and Society, 25*, 119–126. https://doi.org/10.1016/j.emospa.2016.12.003

Tuccille, J. D. (2021, October 12). *Entrepreneurship is on the rise, despite COVID-19*. Reason. https://reason.com/2021/12/10/entrepreneurship-is-on-the-rise-despite-covid-19/

Vallerand, R. J., Blanchard, C., Mageau, G. A., Koestner, R., Ratelle, C., Leonard, M., Gagne, M., & Marsolais, J. (2003). Les passions de l'ame: on obsessive and harmonious passion. *Journal of Personality and Social Psychology, 85*(4), 756–767. https://doi.org/10.1037/0022-3514.85.4.756

Vallerand, R. J., & Houlfort, N. (2019). *Passion for work: Theory, research and applications*. Oxford University Press.

Vallerand, R. J., Paquet, Y., Philippe, F. L., & Charest, J. (2010). On the role of passion for work in burnout: A process model. *Journal of Personality, 78*, 289–312. https://doi.org/10.1111/j.1467-6494.2009.00616.x

Yukhymenko-Lescroart, M. A., & Sharma, G. (2022). Passion for work and well-being of working adults. *Journal of Career Development*, *49*(3), 505–518.

Zayaruzny, D., & Hoa, K. (2023). "Lying Flat": The demise of the Chinese workforce and its impact on the Chinese economy. *Berkeley Economic Review*. https://econreview.studentorg.berkeley.edu/lying-flat-the-demise-of-the-chinese-workforce-and-its-impact-on-the-chinese-economy/.

Zhang, Z., & Li, K. (2023). So you choose to "lie flat?" "Sang-ness," affective economies, and the "lying flat" movement. *Quarterly Journal of Speech*, *109*(1), 48–69. https://doi.org/10.1080/00335630.2022.2143549

CHAPTER 3

THREE TYPES OF SOCIAL LICENCE TO OPERATE: THE ETHICAL AND OPERATIONAL RISKS OF AUTHENTIC, DECEPTIVE, AND DEFAULT SLO APPROACHES

Hugh Breakey[a], Graham Wood[b] and Charles Sampford[a]

[a]*Griffith University, Australia*
[b]*University of Tasmania, Australia*

ABSTRACT

The 'social licence to operate' (SLO) – referring to community acceptance by critical stakeholders – is an important concept in contemporary business ethics, governance, and risk management. In this chapter, we advance a new conceptual framework, arguing that there are three distinct approaches that companies may adopt with respect to community concerns about operations – and that these give rise to three distinct types *of SLO. An* Authentic SLO *is achieved when the organisation genuinely intends to meet and exceed existing standards and social expectations. We give a 'four Cs' delineation of Authentic SLO, based on four pillars of conduct, consequence, credibility, and connection. The* Deceptive SLO *arises when the organisation approaches community concerns as a public relations and branding exercise and employs manipulative and misleading ethics-washing and green-washing to achieve social acceptance. The* Default SLO *occurs when the organisation relies on a pre-existing presumptive acceptance and aims to avoid all public attention, staying out of sight and out of mind*. While all three approaches can successfully lead to community acceptance (and therefore SLO), the three types of resulting SLO differ markedly in terms of ethical, legal, and operational risks. Ultimately, the type of SLO achieved contributes critically not just to the degree of social acceptance the organisation enjoys, but also to the moral significance and operational resilience of that acceptance.

Keywords: Social licence to operate; social acceptance; operational risk; corporate social responsibility; legitimacy

INTRODUCTION

The 'SLO' is a term widely invoked in discussions and strategies around corporate ethics, organisational legitimacy, and operational risk (Brueckner & Eabrasu, 2018; Demuijnck & Fasterling, 2016; Gunningham et al., 2004; Joyce & Thomson, 2002; Santiago et al., 2021). The term initially arose in the late 1990s in the context of operational risk for extraction operations in developing countries (Boutilier & Thomson, 2011; Cooney, 2017; Joyce & Thomson, 2002). Local communities, often supported by international civil society organisations, began protesting and resisting nearby mining operations that impacted on their environment, wellbeing, and livelihood. Mining businesses realised that this resistance posed a risk that operations could be disrupted, or their profits reduced. Thus, as well as a legal licence and political support (from national or state governments), they also needed a *social* licence – support or at least acceptance by the local community (Brueckner & Eabrasu, 2018; Cooney, 2017). The term is now applied beyond the mining sector to many industries and even public works, including aquaculture, forestry, pulp and paper manufacturing, fisheries, tourism, and rail infrastructure (see, e.g., Alexander & Abernethy, 2019; Gunningham et al., 2004; Moffat et al., 2016; Voyer & van Leeuwen, 2018).

This chapter innovates by arguing that attention needs to be given to not just the question of *whether* an organisation has SLO but *what type of* SLO the organisation enjoys. We argue that there are three main approaches organisations can take to SLO concerns, giving rise to three different types of SLO. Organisations can decide to conscientiously live up to and even exceed their community's ethical expectations, taking an *Authentic SLO approach* and giving rise to an *Authentic SLO*. They can undertake to lie to communities and manipulate government bodies – taking a *Deceptive SLO approach* and giving rise to a *Deceptive SLO*. Or they can make a decision – or even a non-decision – to refrain from engaging publicly at all, and rather to stay out of sight and out of mind, taking a *Default SLO approach* and trusting their pre-existing *Default SLO*. Importantly, we argue that each of these three types of SLO gives rise to very different ethical and operational risk profiles, meaning that even an organisation with a high level of community support (and a seemingly strong SLO) might face enormous and irreversible legal and operational risks from a sudden shift in community attitude.

The chapter's argument proceeds as follows. The following section defines the SLO and observes the different gradations of community sentiment (from active resistance to support and pride) towards companies. The next section details the three SLO approaches (Authentic, Deceptive, and Default) that lead to holding each of the three types of SLO. The last section considers the ethical and operational risks posed by each type of SLO.

UNDERSTANDING SLO

For our purposes here, we will understand SLO as referring to the *ongoing acceptance of operations by local community members and other influential stakeholders who can impact on those operations and their profitability*. This definition captures the main features of influential SLO definitions (Cooney, 2017; Famiyeh et al., 2020, p. 435; Joyce & Thomson, 2002; Moffat & Zhang, 2014, p. 61; Santiago et al., 2021): the centrality of social acceptance, the specifying of key stakeholder groups, and the fact (suggested by the term 'licence') that there are material stakes involved: an organisation faces operational and financial risks if it loses acceptance across these stakeholders. These 'SLO risks' (or 'legitimacy penalties' as Jeong & Kim, 2019, p. 1584, term them) may take different forms. Widespread loss of social acceptance across critical stakeholders can give rise to SLO risks in the form of: disruptive protests, legal challenges, product boycotts, personnel impacts, interference with supply chains and product distribution, pushback from socially responsible investors and – above all – major changes to the regulatory environment such as the denial of legal licences, restrictions on advertising, or a newly assertive regulatory posture (Beddewela & Fairbrass, 2016; Cooney, 2017; Famiyeh et al., 2020; Moffat & Zhang, 2014; Murphy-Gregory, 2018). All these challenges involve, at minimum, substantial administrative (and often legal) costs, requiring executives and managers to focus on dispute resolution rather than core business activities (Jeong & Kim, 2019, p. 1589).

'Social acceptance' is not all-or-nothing, as community support can vary on a continuum from unqualified enthusiasm to unbridled resistance (Alexander & Abernethy, 2019; Baines & Edwards, 2018). Drawing on past SLO 'models' (Boutilier & Thomson, 2011; Gehman et al., 2017), Fig. 3.1 graphically illustrates this continuum, tracing a gradient of community sentiment regarding the organisation's operations. It is an 'overall' metric, and it is consistent with there being varying levels of support across different community groups.

The SLO definition above refers to community *acceptance*. But the term 'acceptance' is ambiguous, and can potentially refer to any attitude from principled toleration to unequivocal support. As Mark Suchman (1995, p. 575) observes, it is crucial to specify whether an organisation seeks active support or merely passive acquiescence (see also, Gehman et al., 2017, p. 300). Importantly, the SLO definition focusses on the *stakes* of community action. These stakes arise only when the community opposes the operations, and not when it is merely ambivalent or ignorant about the operations. For this reason, in the definition of SLO, 'acceptance' refers to any attitude from toleration (where the community may not like

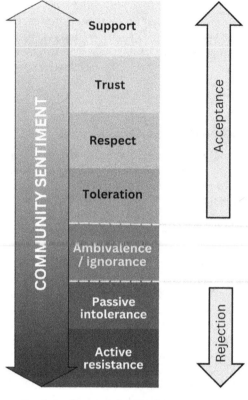

Fig. 3.1 Community Sentiment and Social Acceptance.

the operations, but acknowledges the organisation is entitled to do them) all the way up to the community trusting the operators and supporting them (as shown graphically in Fig. 3.1 by the upward arrow on the right).

Conversely, SLO is lost when the community no longer tolerates the operations. Community intolerance might be passive in cases where it does not accept the operations, but it has not proactively mobilised to disrupt, block, or otherwise sanction the operations or undermine their profitability. (That said, individuals might still undertake passive and isolated activities such as unilaterally avoiding purchasing the organisation's products or using its services. Passive intolerance – if a widespread community sentiment – can therefore impact the organisation's sales and profits.)

Alternatively, the community may move to active resistance, where they begin taking concerted efforts to challenge the operations, such as through protests, leafleting, boycotts, lobbying for immediate government intervention, demanding better enforcement of existing laws, developing legal challenges, and similar activities (Moffat et al., 2016; Murphy-Gregory, 2018). In these cases, the operations are rejected and the SLO has been lost.

There is an important grey area in between where the community is ambivalent about the operations, or simply knows too little about them to form a judgement. In these cases, the organisation has not *lost* its SLO, but neither does it clearly possess SLO.

Because of the damaging potential of SLO risks, businesses are often motivated to respond to ethical issues and community concerns (Beddewela & Fairbrass, 2016; Cooney, 2017). While they might sometimes respond in a straightforwardly pro-social manner (see, e.g., Beddewela & Fairbrass, 2016; Famiyeh et al., 2020), businesses ultimately have a portfolio of alternative approaches they might take to manage such concerns. The next section describes three alternative ways organisations might respond to potential ethical concerns and SLO risks.

THREE TYPES OF SLO

The type of SLO that an organisation holds is a function of the approach it takes to SLO and SLO risks. This section outlines three approaches to SLO that (if used successfully) give rise to three different types of SLO: Authentic, Deceptive, and Default.

Authentic SLO

Organisations adopting an Authentic SLO approach conscientiously try to do the right thing and to be deserving of community support. This organisation is not merely pursuing legitimacy in the sense of ensuring it is socially accepted (Suchman, 1995; Weber, 1919/2007). Rather, it pursues legitimacy in the stronger sense that the organisation and its operations genuinely accord with community values, consent, standards, and expectations (Beetham, 1991; Brueckner & Eabrasu, 2018).

Interestingly, this Authentic SLO approach was invoked in one of the earliest invocations of the term, which provides an example of the approach. In a trade publication, W. Henson Moore (1996), President of the American Forest and Paper Association, outlined the American paper industry's proactive environmental policies. He argued the industry's independently verified achievements could persuade the public that the industry merited their trust. This would result, he argued, in the industry enjoying an 'SLO'.

Like other ethical and corporate social responsibility initiatives, the Authentic SLO approach may be undertaken by an organisation for several different reasons (Beddewela & Fairbrass, 2016, pp. 506–507, 517–518; Famiyeh et al., 2020, pp. 433–436; Jeong & Kim, 2019, p. 1585). It may be motivated by normative and community-based concerns, such as an intrinsic concern for doing the right thing and looking after the long-term security of the organisation's reputation. It may also be adopted strategically, to sustainably avoid serious SLO risks. Finally, it might arise 'mimetically' as an organisation emulates successful exemplars in its industry (Beddewela & Fairbrass, 2016, p. 506; Famiyeh et al., 2020, p. 434).

What does adopting an Authentic SLO approach involve? Early SLO 'models' tied public perceptions of specific ethical behaviours to correlating social outcomes, where a certain type of perceived ethical quality leads to a particular level of acceptance (Boutilier & Thomson, 2011; Gehman et al., 2017). These models helpfully foreground that various types of behaviours and qualities – like trustworthiness – are very important contributors to social acceptance. Along with further research on the determinants of social acceptance (e.g. Alexander & Abernethy, 2019; Voyer & van Leeuwen, 2018), they illustrate that stakeholders will evaluate an institution's acceptability on the basis of an array of moral and contextual considerations.

Building on this research, we advance here a 'four C's' account of Authentic SLO. This account is based on normative accounts of legitimacy – that is, ethical analyses of the key factors justifying the organisation's operations (Breakey, 2022). As well, it incorporates social science (and operational risk) literature and case studies on the factors that impact social acceptance (Alexander &

Abernethy, 2019; Baines & Edwards, 2018; Beetham, 1991; Boutilier & Thomson, 2011; Brucker, 2009; Gehman et al., 2017; Joyce & Thomson, 2002; Voyer & van Leeuwen, 2018).

The four Cs are conduct, consequence, credibility, and connection (see Fig. 3.2).

Conduct concerns how the organisation behaves. It should conform to socially expected norms. If it deals with animals, it should attend to their welfare. It should show respect to stakeholders. It should engage appropriately with third parties, government, media organisations, professional organisations, regulatory agencies, and researchers (e.g. environmental scientists). All these institutions and actors can, at times, take actions that may restrict the organisation's activities or profits, or undermine its brand or level of social acceptance. While perhaps frustrating for the organisation, these actions are often legitimate and arise from the institution playing its proper role in a larger integrity system. An 'integrity system' refers to the overall combination and interaction of institutions and norms in a given context that contributes to an organisation behaving ethically and living up to the standards that justify its existence (Sampford, 2009; Sampford et al., 2005). Responding critically but constructively to these interventions (e.g. scientific or non-governmental organisation, NGO, concern about environmental impacts) may be appropriate. However, attempts to undermine, silence, control, or co-opt these entities is a classic way to fail the requirements of conduct.

Consequence refers to the impact that the organisation has on stakeholders and the environment. Almost all businesses have *some* good consequences: they create employment, they contribute to the local economy (through suppliers, distributors, etc.), they create goods and services that people desire, and by paying taxes they contribute to government revenue. It is a basic expectation that businesses achieve these pro-social outcomes, but at the same time, these achievements filter into the presumptive social acceptance that most businesses enjoy (see below

Fig. 3.2 The Four Cs of Authentic SLO.

'Default SLO'). Businesses can go beyond these expectations to deliver further pro-social consequences. Perhaps they produce renewable energy and so contribute to carbon mitigation efforts. Perhaps they provide locally sourced protein and so contribute to food security. Perhaps they create jobs and economic investment in rural, regional, and remote areas, or for marginalised communities. All these types of pro-social impacts, and many more besides, will improve the organisation's Authentic SLO – especially when the community perceives that the benefits created are being shared fairly (Joyce & Thomson, 2002).

Unfortunately, business operations can also have undesirable consequences for stakeholders and the environment. The operations may be unsustainable, destructive for local ecosystems, or carry unacceptable risks of serious environmental accidents. They may impact local infrastructure, crowding and deteriorating waterways, ports, and roads. They may impact a public resource, interfering with other (perhaps longstanding) users, who engage with the resource for recreational or cultural purposes. They may create visual, noise, or chemical pollution. Consequence requires enhancing the organisation's pro-social effects, and reducing or mitigating any destructive impacts or risks.

Credibility covers the all-important quality of trustworthiness. The organisation should be honest in its claims. It should fulfil its undertakings and promises. It should accept and even welcome mechanisms that make it more accountable (such as forms of transparency and certification). While some information is rightly confidential, the organisation should be frank whenever possible: nothing enhances genuine trust like being upfront about challenges and failures.

Connection involves the organisation engaging constructively with key stakeholders, especially locals and those whose activities are impacted by the organisation (e.g. co-users of a resource). Constructive engagement sometimes involves providing information to the public. If there are good news stories or important new scientific reports, then it is appropriate that these are shared with the community. It is also important to manage expectations, making sure the public is aware of changes that will impact them. However, it involves far more than this, and an all-too-common way of failing connection is to envisage it as a simple one-way flow of information from a knowledgeable organisation to an ignorant public. Instead, connection requires genuinely consulting with community members and listening to their concerns, and – at least at certain times and for certain issues – allowing a level of participation in decision-making (such as negotiating industry limitations to create space for recreational uses of a resource; Alexander & Abernethy, 2019). Community involves being a good neighbour, and ideally being 'part of the community'. It requires building genuine relationships rather than adopting a transactional stance in community interactions (Baines & Edwards, 2018; Williams et al., 2007).

Ultimately, attending to the many elements of the four Cs will require time, effort, investment, leadership, and expertise, adding up to what Jeong and Kim (2019, p. 1584) call a 'legitimacy management cost'. Naturally, organisations must make sensible decisions about their priorities, earnestly pursuing their Authentic SLO ambitions alongside their other operational goals. Even a conscientious organisation may make mistakes, as an ethical business must attend to many different areas of concern (Maak, 2008), and weigh up carefully the legitimacy management costs of different initiatives. However, the organisation's credibility and trustworthiness, its conduct towards other integrity system elements (like media, regulators, and NGOs), and its continued willingness to engage with concerned stakeholders limit the impact that any missteps have on community acceptance.

Deceptive SLO

Deceptive SLO occurs when an organisation aims to actively mislead the public about its actual impacts and practices. This organisation is aware of SLO risks, and therefore acknowledges that social acceptance is (at least somewhat) important to its profits and operations, and cannot be ignored. However, the organisation observes that *deserving* social acceptance is not the only way of *achieving* social acceptance. For the Deceptive SLO approach, the aim is to continue maximising profit as much as possible – including through illegal, unethical, and unsustainable practices – but to achieve social acceptance through manipulating public opinion, and avoiding effective oversight.

The Deceptive SLO approach might present as a strategically desirable option in cases, where (a) the organisation leaders see no independent reason for living up to a community's moral standards (they do not share its values or think they are relevant to its decision-making), and, (b) the organisation leaders believe that pursuing SLO through manipulation and misdirection is a more reliable, realistic, competitive, or cost-effective strategy for managing SLO risk than genuine ethical reform.

There are many well-known ways a Deceptive SLO approach can be undertaken, as the approach aims to make it seem as if the organisation is attending to all the Authentic approach's four Cs. 'Green-washing' refers to the practice of using marketing, advertising, and slick public relations to make operations or products appear to be environmentally sustainable when they are not. Similarly, 'ethics-washing' involves using strategies to trick stakeholders into believing the organisation's conduct and impacts are ethically appropriate, and even laudable. Deceptive SLO includes cultivating influencers, political friends, and media allies to head off public criticism and encourage the organisation's desired framing of events and issues. It can involve capturing or weakening regulators and other gate-keepers (Coffee, 2002). It will pressure in-house and contracted professionals like lawyers and accountants to bend or break their ethical codes to serve the organisation. It will make efforts to silence or de-legitimise complainants (an illustrative array of these strategies can be found in Hayne, 2019). The Deceptive SLO approach will eschew genuine ethical reform (though it might undertake facile initiatives to give the appearance of reform) and instead focus its efforts on slick public relations and misleading (or, if necessary, undermining) government, regulators, and journalistic media.

While adopting the Deceptive SLO approach may seem like a hard-nosed strategic choice, it must be emphasised that it is not always the best decision even from an entirely profit-driven perspective (e.g. strategic action may involve genuinely worthwhile CSR activities: see Beddewela & Fairbrass, 2016). Indeed, pursuing the Deceptive SLO can ultimately prove catastrophic from an operational perspective.

A recent example of Deceptive SLO may be found in the approach used by Purdue Pharma with its drug Oxycontin. Using Oxycontin's time-release system, Purdue intended that the product would be prescribed for chronic pain (Edgell, 2020, p. 260). This strategy faced enormous problems, including doctors' conservatism about prescribing opioids for chronic pain, and the product's vulnerability to more stringent regulations (Edgell, 2020, p. 261). The evidence suggests that the approach Purdue adopted was to influence doctors to falsely believe in the product's safety and efficacy, and more broadly to tap into, and clandestinely assist, a movement in medical ethics to alleviate pain more aggressively, especially in veterans and older adults (Edgell, 2020, pp. 267–270; Yakubi et al., 2022, p. 458). Crucially, US pharmaceutical companies like Purdue found they could sidestep medical advertising restrictions by exploiting non-government bodies and ostensibly independent experts for their marketing purposes, while suppressing their financial links to these (Yakubi et al., 2022, p. 466).

In the short term, these activities were successful and profitable. Purdue and Oxycontin initially had widespread social acceptance, especially across the most important stakeholders: the medical community (Edgell, 2020, pp. 268–269). Voices airing concerns about addiction and abuse were effectively silenced, isolated, or bought off. But the apparent strength of this early social licence belied the fraught nature of how it had been achieved. For all its work, Purdue could only purchase a Deceptive SLO – an outcome that exposed it to extraordinary corporate risk. Its driving focus on combatting and controlling community voices distracted attention from the substantive question of *whether the concerns about high addiction rates were real*, and – if so – the likely (and, arguably, inevitable) long-term consequences of this fact for the company and its drug. In the event, this risk ultimately manifested, leading to the company's collapse and billion-dollar settlements (Edgell, 2020). The collapse shows that companies need to be clear-eyed about the *type* of SLO they are aiming to acquire, and the ethical, legal, operational, and financial risks of doing so. Eschewing genuine ethical reform and response can be strategically disastrous.

Default SLO

Almost all organisations will possess some level of presumptive social acceptance that can help shield them from SLO costs and disruptions. This pre-existing acceptance can arise in two ways.

First, an organisation will normally possess at least some level of moral acceptance – that is, an implicit community view that the organisation is morally entitled to exist and operate (this acceptance might be termed 'moral legitimacy' or 'social legitimacy'; Gehman et al., 2017; Suchman, 1995; Weber, 1919/2007). This moral acceptance can stem from an organisation being established and behaving in accordance with the relevant laws and regulations. At least in a democracy, these rules should be responsive to major and ongoing community concerns and values. Provided that government decision-making and regulatory oversight are perceived by the community to be reasonable and effective, this will supply a strong reason to accept business activities (Alexander & Abernethy, 2019, pp. 10–11).

Moral acceptance can also arise from an organisation performing expected business-as-usual behaviour. A business pays tax, employs locals, creates products or services that are desirable (at least to those who purchase them), brings money into the local economy, and so on. These pro-social activities and outcomes grant businesses a presumptive moral acceptance. An acceptance that the business is entitled to operate might also arise from a view that, at least to some extent, and provided they aren't harming anyone, a business owner is entitled to use their own property in whatever way they choose (Nozick, 1974, p. 171).

Second, the organisation might enjoy 'cognitive legitimacy'. Cognitive legitimacy arises from an organisation simply being present in its location for a long time, or part of a long-established industry, or 'mimetically' doing the same things as other similar organisations, such that it has become part of the furniture of life (Beddewela & Fairbrass, 2016; Famiyeh et al., 2020, p. 434). The organisation aligns with people's expectations, it is understandable and comprehensible to them, and it looks and behaves like other accepted organisations (Long & Driscoll, 2008; Suchman, 1995, pp. 582–584). Perhaps the organisation is so widely taken for granted that its legitimacy is hardly ever consciously considered. (In contrast, *new* industries and operations rarely possess cognitive legitimacy; they suffer a 'liability of newness'; Suchman, 1995, p. 586; Voyer & van Leeuwen, 2018, pp. 16–18.)

As a result, businesses normally enjoy a presumptive social acceptance. While they may not clearly possess a social licence, they may at least be confident that they haven't *lost* it yet (i.e. they are residing in the 'ambivalent' or 'unaware' areas of community sentiment in Fig. 3.1). This allows a third type of SLO practice, one that avoids engaging in SLO activities, eschewing both Authentic SLO genuine ethical reform and engagement and Deceptive SLO manipulative spin and public relations efforts. This non-activity characterises the Default SLO approach. It is particularly appealing to businesses and industries that are long established and have substantial cognitive legitimacy, or are non-public-facing, and largely invisible to the public (as distinct from more exposed and 'closely watched' industries; Gehman et al., 2017, p. 297), or are operating on public resources or lands (Baines & Edwards, 2018, p. 143), or have lost public trust and are unlikely to regain it with altruistic initiatives (Jeong & Kim, 2019, p. 1590).

This Default SLO approach of keeping a low profile can be a deliberate and self-conscious decision: the organisation elects to not rock the boat, and to stay out of sight and out of mind. As Suchman (1995, p. 594) observes: 'Legitimation projects (particularly proactive attempts at advertising, proselytization, and popularization) usually attract attention, and often this attention proves hostile …'. In Voyer and van Leeuwen's (2018, p. 28) report on SLO to the World Ocean Council, a participant observed the shipping industry's resistance to raising the sector's profile, suggesting that the low levels of public scrutiny helped shield the sector from potential SLO issues. In such cases, the Default SLO approach is intentionally chosen.

However, reliance on the Default SLO can also arise from other sorts of decisions – or even non-decisions. Both the Authentic SLO and Deceptive SLO approaches require time, money, effort, and expertise. An organisation might not possess the resources to pursue these approaches. Sometimes these approaches might require the existence of institutional bodies (like industry peak bodies), which may not exist, or might be under-resourced (Alexander & Abernethy, 2019).

Alternatively, the organisation might believe (possibly accurately, possibly mistakenly) that they have no need for work and investment in securing greater community acceptance, perhaps because there is little historical record of operational risk arising from lost social acceptance in that industry. Or the organisation might see its existing social acceptance as rendering it 'bullet proof', obviating any need for proactive strategies (Alexander & Abernethy, 2019, p. 20). Alexander and Abernathy (2019) discuss a case study in Australia where commercial fishers avoided community engagement, and felt they had little need to compromise given their legal right to fish (pp. 20–22). When recreational fishers ran a public campaign against the commercial fishers, the latter's practice of staying out of the spotlight (Alexander & Abernethy, 2019, p. 21) left it with little countervailing social capital.

The Default SLO is thus characterised by a lack of SLO activities. The organisation pursues business-as-normal and avoids public attention as far as possible.

Authentic, Deceptive, and Default SLO Are Each Broad Approaches, and Mixed Approaches Are Possible

The three SLO approaches represent overall stances in engaging with SLO. Such approaches will rarely be present in an unqualified way where *everything* the organisation does follows the general approach. Instead, an organisation might largely adopt one approach, but in specific cases respond in a different way. Three types of complexities are worth noting.

First, even within a single leader or small group of executives, there may be some decisions that diverge from the overall approach. For example, even in an organisation otherwise pursuing a Deceptive SLO approach, there may be some genuine ethical reforms that are forced upon it – reforms that would align better with an Authentic SLO approach. This might occur because these reforms are 'low hanging fruit' or perhaps because the organisation itself doesn't benefit from a certain type of unethical behaviour (such as risk-taking and corner-cutting by low-level employees), and the executive is therefore motivated to genuinely improve compliance that prevents this behaviour. Similarly, a Default SLO approach that prefers not to attract attention may still work hard on one or two ethical areas it recognises as important. For example, in the example mentioned above in 'Default SLO', while the commercial fishers largely stayed out of public view, they genuinely strived (taking a more Authentic SLO approach) to achieve independent certification of the environmental sustainability of their fishing practices (Alexander & Abernethy, 2019, p. 19).

Second, even if there is overall executive support for one approach, at other levels employees might act in ways that are inconsistent with this approach. For example, the executive might be committed to an Authentic SLO approach, but there may be a prevailing culture in some parts of the organisation that resists this approach, and steadfastly continues (and continues covering up) its unethical behaviour (Schein & Schein, 2019).

Third, there may be contestation and change over time. An organisation that adopts a Deceptive SLO approach might find new and continuing employees start to believe and commit to the inspiring ethical values that the organisation (duplicitously) invokes – and begin holding the organisation to those values. Alternatively, an organisation using an Authentic SLO approach might find its community engagement practices (connection) gradually degrade into manipulative public relations, with the focus slowly shifting to controlling the discourse and sidelining contrary voices.

All that said, one approach or another other will tend to predominate, because while each can occasionally include elements of the other, they remain distinct approaches. Adopting one approach will usually make utilising other approaches more challenging and even counterproductive. For example, the Authentic SLO approach involves proactively taking action and engaging with the community – direct opposites of the passive and isolated Default SLO approach. The Authentic SLO approach also will refuse to manipulate, lie, or intimidate community members, or to corrupt or capture political or regulatory bodies – the central strategies of the Deceptive SLO approach. While an organisation employing a Deceptive SLO approach might occasionally 'lie low' on an issue, it generally opposes the isolation and passivity of the Default SLO approach, preferring to stay in the limelight and aggressively maintain control over messaging and branding. Similarly, the Deceptive SLO approach might occasionally adopt a particular ethical initiative, but because of its prevailing approach, it will rarely have the organisational culture or compliance systems required to deliver and sustain ethical initiatives. In short, the effectiveness of each approach tends to crowd out adopting the others.

Perceptions of SLO Approaches by Those Inside and Outside the Organisation

The SLO approach adopted by an organisation may not be easily visible to outsiders – that is, to stakeholders outside the organisation. To be sure, an organisation's Default SLO approach is usually easy to perceive, even by outsiders, as the organisation largely avoids any activity that draws attention to its moral standing or performance. In contrast, for an external observer, accurately perceiving an organisation's Deceptive SLO approach can be difficult. After all, the whole point of the Deceptive SLO approach is to *look like* the Authentic SLO approach. Sometimes, it will even be possible that internal observers (like employees) aren't aware of the organisation's overall approach. They may work following the culture in their own part of the organisation, not realising that behaviour differs markedly from the direction of other parts of the organisation. Alternatively, employees might be well aware that its public branding does not reflect its actual practice.

DISCUSSION: ETHICAL AND OPERATIONAL RISK PROFILES OF SLO TYPES

Relationship Between SLO Type and Level of Social Acceptance

Adopting a particular SLO approach does not guarantee holding an SLO, or attaining a particular level of social acceptance (such as trusted, supported, or tolerated). No SLO approach – not even the Authentic SLO approach that aims to genuinely live up to and exceed community standards – can guarantee a particular level of social acceptance. Case studies on social acceptance show that – while the four Cs cover most of the social acceptance determinants within the organisation's control – unexpected events and fickle community attitudes do play a role in delivering social acceptance (Alexander & Abernethy, 2019; Melé & Armengou, 2016; Murphy-Gregory, 2018).

Nevertheless, different SLO approaches will tend to aim at different levels of social acceptance, putting a 'ceiling' on how powerful their social acceptance is likely to be, even in a best-case scenario (see Fig. 3.3).

The Authentic SLO approach will normally aim to achieve more than passive acceptance. Because the organisation aims to genuinely live up to community standards, it would expect to achieve the higher levels of acceptance, including respect, trust, and support, as illustrated in Fig. 3.3.

In contrast, the Default SLO approach can only aim to achieve the passive acceptance that an organisation can (at best) possess purely on the basis of being a law-abiding business. Anything greater than this level would require drawing public attention to themselves. Even more minimally, an organisation adopting the Default SLO approach could be satisfied with achieving 'Unawareness', where the community simply does not know enough about the organisation and its practices to have any opinion on its acceptability. This low level of acceptance may be enough to allow the organisation to reliably keep on operating with business-as-usual.

The Deceptive SLO approach can aim for any

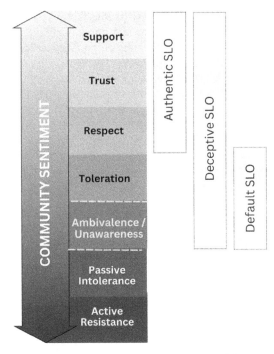

Fig. 3.3 Social Acceptance Targeted by SLO Approaches.

level of public acceptance. If the strategic goal is just to avoid costly disruptions and aggressive government interventions, then it may aim for no more than passive acceptance (or even more minimally, ambivalence). However, if there are reasons of branding and other benefits that would accrue from wider public acceptance, then higher levels may be pursued. Indeed, because it focusses so directly on branding and image, the Deceptive SLO approach may even succeed in cultivating strong social support and brand loyalty, where the organisation has cultivated such a beguiling image that others are keen to associate with it.

The Different Ethical Risk Profiles of the Three SLO Approaches

The Authentic SLO approach raises only minimal ethical risks. Conduct and consequence require attending to the ethical cause of social concerns, rather than the symptoms (community resistance) that might ultimately arise. Credibility is itself ethical, requiring honesty and respecting the community's informed consent to the organisation's operations. Connection means keeping a finger on the pulse of community concerns, and therefore being forewarned about any looming ethical issues that must be navigated.

The Default SLO approach carries a varied (and sometimes unknown) amount of ethical risk. An organisation may be profoundly unethical and therefore aim to keep out of sight of public and media precisely for this reason. Alternatively, the organisation might take ethical concerns and sustainability seriously, but otherwise aim to keep a low profile. Yet, even this latter approach carries ethical risks, as it does not have the public visibility and communication systems that allow it to be aware of rising community concerns and the ethical issues that are prompting those concerns.

The Deceptive SLO approach carries enormous ethical risks – indeed, it actively involves violating ethical principles. First, the Deceptive SLO is only undertaken when the organisation is performing operations or having effects that it knows would not meet with community approval. But second, the Deceptive SLO approach actively worsens the moral situation by trying to cover up these concerns, and engaging in unjustifiable activities like misleading the public, silencing critics, and corrupting regulators. The Deceptive SLO approach thus requires the organisation to double down on its existing ethical failures.

The Different Operational Risk Profiles of the Three SLO Approaches

In terms of operational risk, decision-makers will want to know the *resilience* of their current community acceptance and SLO. Granted, things are fine now, but could everything change overnight?

The resilience of an organisation's SLO depends on its SLO type. This is a complexity that must be borne in mind when an organisation's SLO is being evaluated or measured (Gehman et al., 2017, pp. 305–309).

The Default SLO is vulnerable because the first scandal or ethical challenge encountered is the first thing the public learns about the organisation. The public knew little about the organisation and its challenges, so it was not expecting the scandal. Worse, the public has no countervailing knowledge of the goods and values the organisation creates that could counterbalance its newfound awareness of the organisation's problems. It may also be that opposition to the organisation has gradually been growing and becoming more organised while the organisation maintained its low-profile approach. When problems arise, there are no established support networks or social capital the organisation can rely on, and it can be too late to build the necessary support to survive (as occurred in the above-mentioned case study by Alexander & Abernethy, 2019, pp. 15–25). A separate danger is that the industry with a Default SLO might not realise how exposed it is to social licence risks. Because it successfully stays outside the spotlight, it might not have a clear awareness of the consequences that might ensue from having community, media, and political attention suddenly focussed on the organisation's operations, and might not have plans or systems to respond effectively to this attention.

The Default SLO is therefore only resilient in cases where visible ethical challenges, costly accidents, or major scandals are extremely unlikely, or where the organisation or industry is so socially vital that it can withstand the spotlight being trained upon it.

The Deceptive SLO avoids this vulnerability by cultivating allies and controlling institutions (like universities, researchers, media, regulators, and political parties). It has built up its social capital over time through effective public relations campaigns that have showcased its (real or confected) socially beneficial impacts, and downplayed, re-framed, or de-legitimised its social risks and costs. When an SLO issue arises, it might be able to rely on these resources to weather the storm.

The real risk for the Deceptive SLO is that its underhanded manipulations – its tactic of adopting the Deceptive SLO approach itself – are exposed. Once its efforts at regulatory capture, bribing constituents, covering up problems, or silencing complainants come to light, the public will now be wary about all those good news stories and suspicious of the allies supporting the organisation. They will wonder what else they aren't being told. They will wonder whether these 'allies' have simply been bought. Indeed, at moments like these, allies might suddenly desert the organisation, fearful of the effect their association will have on *their own* social standing (Suchman, 1995, p. 597).

Once social acceptance falters for the Deceptive SLO, it is enormously hard to rebuild. Because the organisation has been caught manipulating public opinion, the public will naturally wonder if the latest round of apologies, lessons-learned, staff turnovers, and proposed reforms are simply more of the same misdirection. Pursuing the Deceptive SLO approach thus carries special operational risks. While a Deceptive SLO might allow the organisation to survive the occasional ethical scandal, once things start going wrong, problems may cascade in an unstoppable unravelling.

Arguably, the Purdue Pharma case described above provides an example of the fragility of even strong levels of acceptance when they are achieved through the Deceptive SLO approach. As described above, during the early years of Oxycontin's rollout, Purdue managed to achieve support and trust among its most crucial stakeholder group: prescribing doctors (Edgell, 2020, pp. 268–269).

Indeed, it even managed to frame attacks on its product as unethical – as based on a callous disregard for human suffering that its product could mercifully alleviate. But Purdue executives would have been tragically mistaken if during this halcyon period they had failed to recognise the enormous and potentially catastrophic operational, legal, and regulatory risks that loomed for the organisation (Edgell, 2020).

While often hard work in the short term, the Authentic SLO is lower risk in the longer term, as this approach builds genuine support and committed allies, and addresses key ethical concerns. However, an Authentic SLO can still be vulnerable, especially if the organisation has not attended to all the elements of the four Cs, and therefore has areas of vulnerability it has not addressed. This vulnerability will be especially so for major new enterprises that enjoy no cognitive legitimacy (e.g. see Melé & Armengou, 2016; Murphy-Gregory, 2018).

CONCLUSION

This chapter's key message is that a crucial question to ask of any organisation is: what is the organisation's *approach* to issues of social acceptance, and (therefore) what *type* of SLO does it hold? Crucially, even if an organisation enjoys widespread levels of support and trust, its SLO might be fragile, meaning that despite its current support it faces potentially enormous legal, operational, and financial risks. This will be especially the case for organisations that adopt a Deceptive SLO approach, where high rates of social acceptance might unravel quickly and irreversibly when its deceptions are revealed. An organisation possessing a Default SLO can also be vulnerable, as it will not have built up social capital and community connections that could help it endure a sudden scandal or controversy.

Ultimately, from both an ethical perspective and an operational risk perspective, not all social licences are equal. There are good reasons – both ethical and operational – for organisations to adopt an Authentic SLO approach.

ACKNOWLEDGEMENTS

The authors acknowledge the financial support of the Blue Economy Cooperative Research Centre (CRC), established and supported under the Australian Government's CRC Programme, grant number CRC-20180101. The CRC Programme supports industry-led collaborations between industry, researchers, and the community. This research was funded through the project 'Ethics, Values, and Social Licence in the Blue Economy' (Project 5.20.005). The authors particularly wish to thank Project Steering Group members David Rissik, Ian Dutton, Jonathan Fievez, Sean Riley, Graham Wood, and Marcus Haward. The authors would also like to acknowledge the input of Rebecca Marshallsay and the constructive comments of two anonymous reviewers.

REFERENCES

Alexander, K., & Abernethy, K. (2019). *Determinants of socially-supported wild-catch fisheries and aquaculture in Australia*. Fisheries Research and Development Corporation.

Baines, J., & Edwards, P. (2018). The role of relationships in achieving and maintaining a social licence in the New Zealand aquaculture sector. *Aquaculture, 485*, 140–146.

Beddewela, E., & Fairbrass, J. (2016). Seeking legitimacy through CSR: Institutional pressures and corporate responses of multinationals in Sri Lanka. *Journal of Business Ethics, 136*(3), 503–522.

Beetham, D. (1991). *The legitimation of power*. Macmillan.

Boutilier, R. G., & Thomson, I. (2011). Modelling and measuring the social license to operate: Fruits of a dialogue between theory and practice. *Social License*. Available at: https://socialicense.com/publications/Modelling%20and%20Measuring%20the%20SLO.pdf [Accessed 25 Nov 2024].

Breakey, H. (2022). The comprehensive multidimensional legitimacy model: A methodology for applied ethics evaluation, institutional diagnosis and practical reform initiatives. *Research in Ethical Issues in Organisations, 26*, 93–112.

Brucker, D. (2009). In defense of adaptive preferences. *Philosophical Studies, 142*, 307–324.

Brueckner, M., & Eabrasu, M. (2018). Pinning down the social license to operate (SLO): The problem of normative complexity. *Resources Policy, 59*, 217–226.

Coffee, J. (2002). Understanding enron: "It's about the gatekeepers, stupid". *The Business Lawyer, 57*, 1403–1420.

Cooney, J. (2017). Reflections on the 20th anniversary of the term 'social licence'. *Journal of Energy & Natural Resources Law, 35*, 197–200. https://doi.org/10.1080/02646811.2016.1269472

Demuijnck, G., & Fasterling, B. (2016). The social license to operate. *Journal of Business Ethics, 136*(4), 675–685. https://doi.org/10.1007/s10551-015-2976-7

Edgell, C. (2020). It's time to finish what they started: How Purdue Pharma and the Sackler family can help end the opioid epidemic. *Penn State Law Review, 125*(1), 255–288.

Famiyeh, S., Asante-Darko, D., Kwarteng, A., Gameti, D. K., & Asah, S. A. (2020). Corporate social responsibility initiatives and its impact on social license: Some empirical perspectives. *Social Responsibility Journal, 16*(3), 431–447. https://doi.org/10.1108/SRJ-06-2018-0147

Gehman, J., Lefsrud, L. M., & Fast, S. (2017). Social license to operate: Legitimacy by another name? *Canadian Public Administration, 60*(2), 293–317.

Gunningham, N., Kagan, R. A., & Thornton, D. (2004). Social license and environmental protection: Why businesses go beyond compliance. *Law & Social Inquiry, 29*(2), 307–341. https://doi.org/10.1111/j.1747-4469.2004.tb00338.x

Hayne, K. (2019). *Final report: Royal Commission into misconduct in the banking, superannuation and financial services industry* (Vol. 1). Royal Commission into the Banking, Superannuation and Financial Services Industry.

Jeong, Y.-C., & Kim, T.-Y. (2019). Between legitimacy and efficiency: An institutional theory of corporate giving. *Academy of Management Journal, 62*(5), 1583–1608. https://doi.org/10.5465/amj.2016.0575

Joyce, S., & Thomson, I. (2002). Earning a social licence to operate: Social acceptability and resource development in Latin America. *CIM Bulletin, 93*(1037), 49–53.

Long, B. S., & Driscoll, C. (2008). Codes of ethics and the pursuit of organizational legitimacy: Theoretical and empirical contributions. *Journal of Business Ethics, 77*(2), 173–189, https://doi.org/10.1007/s10551-006-9307-y

Maak, T. (2008). Undivided corporate responsibility: Towards a theory of corporate integrity. *Journal of Business Ethics, 82*, 353–368.

Melé, D., & Armengou, J. (2016). Moral legitimacy in controversial projects and its relationship with social license to operate: A case study. *Journal of Business Ethics, 136*, 729–742.

Moffat, K., Lacey, J., Zhang, A., & Leipold, S. (2016). The social licence to operate: A critical review. *Forestry: An International Journal of Forest Research, 89*(5), 477–488. https://doi.org/10.1093/forestry/cpv044

Moffat, K., & Zhang, A. (2014). The paths to social licence to operate: An integrative model explaining community acceptance of mining. *Resources Policy, 39*, 61–70.

Moore, W. H. (1996). The social license to operate. *PIMA Magazine, 78*(10), 22–23.

Murphy-Gregory, H. (2018). Governance via persuasion: Environmental NGOs and the social licence to operate. *Environmental Politics*, *27*(2), 320–340. https://doi.org/10.1080/09644016.2017.1373429

Nozick, R. (1974). *Anarchy, state, and utopia*. Basil Blackwell.

Sampford, C. (2009). From deep north to international governance exemplar: Fitzgerald's impact on the international anti-corruption movement. *Griffith Law Review*, *18*(3), 559–575.

Sampford, C., Smith, R., & Brown, A. J. (2005). From Greek temple to bird's nest: Towards a theory of coherence and mutual accountability for national integrity systems. *Australian Journal of Public Administration*, *64*(2), 96–108.

Santiago, A. L., Demajorovic, J., Rossetto, D. E., & Luke, H. (2021). Understanding the fundamentals of the social licence to operate: Its evolution, current state of development and future avenues for research. *Resources Policy*, *70*, 101941. https://doi.org/10.1016/j.resourpol.2020.101941

Schein, E., & Schein, P. (2019). *The corporate culture survival guide* (3rd ed.). Wiley.

Suchman, M. C. (1995). Managing legitimacy: Strategic and institutional approaches. *Academy of Management Review*, *20*(3), 571–610.

Voyer, M., & van Leeuwen, J. (2018). *Social license to operate and the blue economy* [Report to World Ocean Council, pp. 1–40]. Australian National Centre for Ocean Resources and Security.

Weber, M. (1919/2007). Politics as a vocation. In J. Dreijmanis (Ed.), *Max Weber's complete writings on academic and political vocations* (pp. 21–42). Algora.

Williams, P., Gill, A., & Ponsford, I. (2007). Corporate social responsibility at tourism destinations: Toward a social license to operate. *Tourism Review International*, *11*, 133–144.

Yakubi, H., Gac, B., & Apollonio, D. E. (2022). Marketing opioids to veterans and older adults: A content analysis of internal industry documents released from State of Oklahoma v. Purdue Pharma LP, et al. *Journal of Health Politics, Policy and Law*, *47*(4), 453–472. https://doi.org/10.1215/03616878-9716712

CHAPTER 4

EVALUATIVE CONSISTENCY AND ETHICAL LEADERSHIP

Jessica Flanigan

Jepson School of Leadership Studies, University of Richmond, VA, USA

ABSTRACT

This chapter argues that political and business leaders should adhere to the same moral standards as everyone else, a position that the author terms Evaluative Consistency. According to this view, there is a single set of moral principles applicable to all individuals, regardless of their leadership roles. This contrasts with Evaluative Exceptionalism, the belief that leadership ethics should be evaluated by a different set of moral standards that do not apply to ordinary decision-makers. The chapter begins by outlining the case for Exceptionalism, which holds that the unique moral challenges faced by leaders necessitate different moral rules, or that the context in which leaders operate justifies a separate ethical framework – or even that leaders may be exempt from moral requirements altogether. Next, the author argues in favor of Consistency and against Exceptionalism, suggesting that the same arguments used to reject Exceptionalism in just war theory should also apply to leaders in business ethics and political philosophy. Subsequent sections address objections to Consistency, including its implications in "dirty hands" scenarios and its compatibility with the distinctive duties of leaders, such as fiduciary responsibilities and confidentiality. Finally, the chapter discusses how Consistency impacts the study and teaching of ethical leadership, concluding with a call to apply uniform moral standards across all roles, including leadership.

Keywords: Exceptionalism; just war theory; leadership; Consistency; business ethics

1. INTRODUCTION

In this chapter, I argue that political and business leaders should act according to the same moral considerations that apply to everyone else. Leadership is not morally distinctive. I call this position Evaluative Consistency, meaning that people should evaluate leadership ethics and ordinary behavior by the same standards. On this view, there is a single set of moral standards that applies to everyone, regardless of whether they occupy a leadership role. Consistency is framed in contrast to Evaluative Exceptionalism, which is the view that people should evaluate leadership ethics by a set of moral standards that do not apply to ordinary decision-makers.

I describe the case for Exceptionalism in Section 2. Exceptionalists may believe that the moral challenges of leadership require a different set of moral rules that leaders operate in a context that means that different moral rules apply to them, or that moral requirements don't apply to leaders at all. There, I draw an analogy between leadership ethics and just war theory. In Section 3, I make the case for Consistency and against Exceptionalism. I argue that the same considerations against Exceptionalism for soldiers in just war theory are also reasons to reject Exceptionalism for leaders in business ethics and political philosophy. In Section 4, I respond to the objection that Consistency has unacceptable implications in dirty hands scenarios. In Section 5, I respond to the objection that Consistency is inconsistent with leaders having distinctive permissions and obligations related to fiduciary duties or confidentiality requirements. In Section 6, I discuss the implications of Consistency for the study and teaching of ethical leadership. Finally, Section 7 concludes.

2. EXCEPTIONALISM

Imagine that someone lied to you or withheld information that you were entitled to know. For example, consider how you would feel if a physician misled you about a medical diagnosis. Now, imagine that the person who lied to you occupied a formal position of authority over you. For example, consider how you would feel if your boss misled you about the potential for layoffs in the next six months. Some scholars of leadership ethics suggest that leaders who occupy formal positions of authority are entitled to deceive people more often than ordinary friends, family members, and service providers. I call this view Exceptionalism because it involves making exceptions to general moral standards of blame and criticism for people who are acting as leaders.

Exceptionalists don't just defend instances of deceptive and manipulative leadership that would otherwise be wrong; they also defend leaders' entitlement to use force and coercion in contexts where they acknowledge that it would be wrong for ordinary people to force or coerce each other. Many political philosophers are Exceptionalists when it comes to public officials. They argue that public officials are entitled to use violence, seize property, and incarcerate people but that ordinary citizens are not. In just war theory, Exceptionalists defend what is sometimes called "orthodox just war theory." This approach to just war theory holds that war is a morally exceptional circumstance that requires different standards of praise, blame, and criticism. So, while it would ordinarily be extremely unethical to kill a person who is defending a just cause, Exceptionalists hold that uniformed combatants may permissibly assault and kill each other during armed conflicts.

In legal contexts, people who occupy formal roles of authority are often granted privileges and immunities that others lack. As I will discuss in Section 5, there are sometimes good pragmatic reasons to hold leaders to different legal standards. Yet, Exceptionalists hold that leaders should be held to different standards because they have different moral obligations and entitlements in virtue of their status as leaders.[1] For example, many leadership scholars argue that leaders should act as moral exemplars or role models who hold themselves to higher ethical standards than others in the organization.[2]

Leadership consultants also implicitly defend Exceptionalism in the way they talk about leadership. For example, when they argue that leaders need different kinds of moral training to prepare them for the tough choices they will encounter, they implicitly suggest that different kinds of moral reasons apply to people in leadership positions.[3]

Even social scientists contribute to the Exceptionalist narrative insofar as they use theoretical and methodological frameworks to study leadership that they do not use for non-leaders. For example, some organizational psychologists use different methods or apply different survey instruments to evaluate leaders.[4] Other leadership scholars single out leaders as moral exemplars or role models.[5]

There are various moral defenses of Exceptionalism in the philosophical literature. Some Exceptionalists believe that the moral challenges of leadership require a different set of moral rules. Robert Goodin suggests a view like this in utilitarianism as a public philosophy. There, Goodin (1995) argues that, while ordinary individuals are morally required to respect each other's enforceable rights against interference, political leaders ought to make decisions based on utilitarian considerations. More recently, Johan Brännmark (2016) has defended a view called "moral disunitarianism," which holds that moral norms are not unified across all contexts. On this view, different moral considerations apply to people who find themselves in different circumstances.

We can also reconstruct a moral case for Exceptionalism by drawing an analogy between Exceptionalism and orthodox just war theory. Orthodox just war theorists, including Michael Walzer (2015), argue that different permitting and requiring moral reasons apply to combatants in wartime scenarios. For example, though it is ordinarily impermissible to kill someone who does not pose a threat to an innocent person, targeting non-threatening combatants in war, for example, by bombing a military base, is permissible. Orthodox theorists have several arguments to defend this view.[6] First, they note that this approach to war has been the dominant approach for centuries, and for good reason. It is usually not psychologically or politically feasible for combatants and commanders to avoid killing in war.[7] Combatants face greater empirical and moral uncertainty than ordinary citizens too, so they should not be expected to take the level of due care in deliberation that we expect from people in peacetime contexts. Additionally, since other combatants are unlikely to comply with demanding ethical principles during a war, a community that held combatants to the fairly demanding moral standards that apply to non-combatants in peacetime contexts would place itself at a serious security disadvantage.

Other orthodox just war theorists have argued that even unjust combatants, meaning soldiers who are fighting for an unjust cause, have duties to protect their compatriots (Lazar, 2013). Sometimes, combatants can consent to the risks of being killed in a war, and this may mitigate the injustice of killing them during wartime. On the other hand, insofar as some combatants' decision to fight is not fully voluntary, this may mitigate the extent to which they are blameworthy for their conduct in war. For this reason, some orthodox theorists argue that even if the same moral considerations that justify or prohibit killing in interpersonal contexts also apply to killing in war, empirical realities and non-ideal theoretic considerations support an approach to killing in war that is very different from the approach that most governments adopt with respect to killing in interpersonal conflicts (Ford, 2022).

The analogy between orthodox just war theory and Exceptionalism in leadership ethics is straightforward.[8] Perhaps because of the similarities between leadership and wartime ethics, some leadership scholars explicitly invoke the language of war to describe ethically fraught leadership situations.[9] Non-military leadership scenarios can also be unusually demanding, high-stakes, and morally risky, so some non-military leadership circumstances might also merit Exceptionalism in ethics.

Consider another analogy from political philosophy. Some political philosophers believe in a concept called political authority.[10] They argue that public officials have the authority to use coercion in contexts where ordinary citizens do not. For example, public officials can coercively collect taxes to provide public goods, but ordinary citizens lack the authority to do this (Klosko, 1987). Other political philosophers are anarchists. They believe that public officials don't have any moral authority that citizens lack. So, if taxation for the sake of public goods is permissible, it's permissible for anyone to do it (Huemer, 2013). If this strikes us as implausible, then we should rethink officials' authority to tax as well. By analogy, Exceptionalists are like theorists of political obligation while Consistency theorists are like anarchists.

In each case, Exceptionalists believe that different moral rules apply to leaders because of the distinctive role they occupy. In defense of Exceptionalism in non-political leadership ethics cases, one could make similar arguments as the defenses of Exceptionalism in other contexts. For example, perhaps it is psychologically or politically infeasible to hold leaders to the same moral standards that apply to everyone else. Or, maybe leaders who hold themselves to the same moral standards that apply to everyone else will put themselves and their organizations at a strategic disadvantage. Leadership is also risky and high-stakes, so leaders face epistemic challenges similar to those faced by combatants in wartime. Moreover, like combatants, leaders have special duties to members of their organization that may lead them to believe that they should protect other members of the organization, even if doing so involves violating some general moral principles.

In the next section, I argue that Exceptionalism in leadership ethics encounters many of the same objections as orthodox just war theory and theories of political obligation. In each of these cases, the case for Consistency is as simple as it is compelling; leaders should be held to the same moral standards as the rest of us.

3. SINGLE STANDARDS

The case against Exceptionalism has three parts. First, I will show that the strongest justifications for Exceptionalism do not support the conclusion that leaders should be held to different moral standards. Second, I will defend Consistency as a morally better approach to leadership. Third, I will make the case for Consistency on pragmatic grounds.

Let's continue with the analogy to just war theory. The main philosophical rival to orthodox just war theory is called revisionist just war theory. Revisionist theorists argue that the same ethical principles that apply to ordinary people during peacetime also apply to combatants in wartime situations.[11] To illustrate the distinction between orthodox just war theorists and revisionists, consider their differing views of the moral equality of combatants. Orthodox just war theorists claim that all combatants are equally liable to be killed in war and equally permitted to kill other combatants in war. Revisionist just war theorists argue that combatants are not liable to be killed in war insofar as they are fighting for a just cause, such as self-defense or the protection of innocent civilians. In contrast, revisionists argue that combatants who are fighting for an unjust cause, threatening others with unwarranted violence, are liable to be killed. Similarly, combatants who fight for a just cause are entitled to use deadly force, but unjust combatants are not.

Jeff McMahan (2009) is the most influential revisionist just war theorist. He argues that soldiers ought to use their own judgment to decide whether they are defending a just or unjust cause. If they are fighting for a just cause, then they have the authority to use deadly force. If they are fighting for an unjust cause, they forfeit their rights against being killed because of the unjust threat they pose to others. McMahan (2004) draws an analogy between a security guard and a bank robber. In the context of a standoff, the guard who is defending innocent customers at the bank is morally entitled to use force and is not liable to be killed. The person who is threatening innocent customers and robbing the bank is not entitled to use force and is liable to be killed. So, too, in wartime scenarios, it matters whether the fighter is acting justly.

McMahan's argument for revisionist just war theory is essentially an argument for a version of Consistency. People who put on a military uniform are not then transported to an entirely new moral landscape. The same standards of permissibility that apply to non-combatants apply on the battlefield, too. Insofar as people have enforceable rights, for example, rights against interference, they have those rights against anyone who might potentially interfere with them. Just combatants don't lose their rights against interference when they happen to be interacting with another soldier. By analogy, the case for Consistency in leadership contexts proceeds similarly. Insofar as people have enforceable rights against force, fraud, coercion, manipulation, killing, privacy violations, theft, or other forms of mistreatment, everyone must respect those rights. People who interact with leaders who occupy formal positions of authority don't have fewer rights than people who interact on a level playing field. So too, leaders do not forfeit their rights when they assume a leadership role.

Or, return to the foregoing analogy to political obligation. Proponents of political obligation sometimes argue that public officials are authorized to use coercion in contexts where ordinary citizens are not, on the grounds that public officials derive their authority from having the support of a majority of citizens (Christiano, 2004). Or, they argue that public officials have the moral authority to compel people to obey the law as long as no one is compelled to comply with a law that a reasonable person would not agree to (Rawls, 2005). Anarchist political philosophers have argued against these views on the grounds that people do not forfeit their rights against being coerced whenever someone else has the support of a majority or follows a procedure before threatening them with violence and incarceration (John Simmons, 1999). To an anarchist, an individual's consent to be interfered with is the only thing that can give a leader the authority to interfere with them in a case where ordinary morality does not permit interference.

Consistency, like philosophical anarchism, is the view that leadership doesn't change the moral landscape regarding people's entitlements and obligations. To the extent that people have enforceable natural rights, leaders are bound to respect the rights of their fellow men, and so is everyone else. This is not to say that people cannot change their rights and obligations to others, for example, by making binding consensual agreements. Consistency only requires that insofar as people have the normative authority to waive their rights or to acquire obligations to others, all people have this normative power regardless of their status as a leader, follower, or bystander. Likewise, if people are owed care and respect, Consistency holds that people are owed this care and respect whether they are leaders or not. Correspondingly, if people have the authority to coerce or if they are liable to be coerced, those standards of authority and liability apply to all their relationships (in the absence of voluntary agreements that grant or waive liability). Leaders are not presumptively entitled to more or less status and consideration than anyone else. So too, leaders owe everyone the same care and respect that each person owes one another.

Consistency, as a structural claim about the nature of leadership ethics, is compatible with various moral theories. Yet, Consistency is not entirely neutral regarding debates in normative ethics. For example, Lazar (2013) argues that people can acquire distinctive permissions and obligations by virtue of their social role, whether they consented to the role or not, which can override their more general moral obligations, including the duty to refrain from violating people's rights.

Evaluative Consistency and Ethical Leadership

This view entails the denial of Consistency. On the other hand, it is less clear whether other accounts of associative obligation entail the denial of Consistency (Scheffler, 1997). For example, it could be that people have unenforceable moral reasons to act by virtue of being in valuable relationships, but that they only have these reasons when acting in accordance with them is consistent with complying with their more general rights and obligations.

Another reason that Consistency is an especially attractive approach to leadership ethics is that Consistency is a presumptively more egalitarian moral theory than Exceptionalism. Assuming that a moral theory is more plausible, all else equal, if it holds everyone subject to the theory to the same standards of permission and obligation, Consistency can more easily meet this desideratum of a moral theory. This is not to say that Exceptionalism is inherently unequal. A proponent of Exceptionalism could argue that as long as everyone has a fair or equal chance of occupying a leadership role, it is not necessarily inegalitarian to hold leaders to either higher or lower moral standards. In contrast, Consistency does not structurally introduce inequalities in the benefits or burdens associated with compliance with an egalitarian moral theory by differentiating between people by virtue of their social position or role. So if, for example, people are required to adopt an egalitarian ethos, to relate to each other as equals, to hold equal power with one another, or to distribute resources to the worst off, Consistency has a presumptive egalitarian advantage.

At this point, I imagine some readers are frustrated by my characterization of the issue because, in arguing that the principles of interpersonal morality should apply equally to leaders, I am assuming that there are some true universal principles of interpersonal morality. This claim strikes some people as controversial because we do not know what interpersonal morality requires. After all, people disagree about the scope and content of people's enforceable rights, whether welfare rights exist, what respect requires, what kind of equality is morally important, and whether people are obligated to care for the needy and vulnerable. Yet, the fact that people disagree about the demands of interpersonal morality suggests that they think that there is some truth of the matter – that is why they are disagreeing![12] Most people agree about at least some aspects of interpersonal morality, such as the claim that "it is wrong to kill someone who is morally innocent and non-threatening." My aim in this chapter is not to describe a full moral theory but only to defend the view that interpersonal morality, whatever it requires, applies to leaders with equal moral force. In this sense, I am defending a limited claim about the structure of morality rather than a broader claim about the content of our moral obligations and entitlements.

Moreover, to the extent that moral skepticism is a problem for Consistency, it is a problem for Exceptionalists as well. Both proponents of Consistency and Exceptionalism make moral claims about the relationship between everyday moral requirements and leadership ethics. If anything, Exceptionalists face a higher justificatory burden on this dimension because their view requires them to defend not only a theory of interpersonal morality, but a separate moral theory for leaders too.

Of course, just as people are uncertain about what morality requires in particular cases, they may also be uncertain about whether Exceptionalism or Consistency is justified. Each position is controversial because Consistency and Exceptionalism have revisionary implications for how we think about leadership ethics. For example, Consistency challenges the widespread intuition that public officials, in virtue of their role, have special permissions and obligations to use force or to coerce people. Yet, Exceptionalism challenges the intuition that moral reasons and requirements apply to everyone equally, regardless of their social position.

But even if one is uncertain about whether leaders are subject to different moral rules, there are also pragmatic reasons to endorse Consistency in leadership ethics. For one thing, moral failure in leadership often arises because leaders mistakenly think that moral rules do not apply to them (Price, 2000). The rhetoric of Exceptionalism could make leaders more prone to this kind of ethical failure by promoting the message that ordinary moral rules do not apply to leaders without then specifying the leader-centric moral requirements that do apply to them. So, for pragmatic reasons, scholars and leadership educators who are uncertain about whether Consistency or Exceptionalism is the right view of leadership ethics may reasonably hedge against the risk of moral skepticism and encourage leaders to abide by the moral requirements and reasons that apply in interpersonal contexts.[13]

4. DIRTY HANDS

Proponents of Exceptionalism may object that Consistency has unacceptable implications in situations where abiding by universal moral standards would result in a serious moral catastrophe. Sometimes, these are called "dirty hands" cases. In this section, I will first describe why these cases seemingly pose a challenge to Consistency before arguing that they actually reveal a more general challenge for all moral theorizing. Dirty hands cases raise difficult ethical issues, but these issues are orthogonal to debates about Exceptionalism versus Consistency.

Dirty hands cases arise when leaders must decide whether to violate rights or some other strongly held moral requirement in order to avoid a moral catastrophe (Coady, 2024). In addition to defending orthodox just war theory, Michael Walzer (2015) coined the term and appealed to the concept of dirty hands in justifying the allied bombings of German civilians during World War 2.

In contrast to some leadership theorists, proponents of both Consistency and Exceptionalism agree that ethical considerations do apply to leaders in dirty hands situations.[14] Proponents of Consistency hold that leaders don't get a special pass to violate rights when the stakes are high (Waldron, 2005). Proponents of Exceptionalism hold that it is permissible for leaders to violate moral requirements during emergencies or that, in these cases, leaders have decisive moral reasons to violate moral requirements for the sake of the greater good. Proponents of Exceptionalism needn't claim that leaders are obligated to violate rights in these cases, though some do. If dirty hands leadership is not required and if leaders have prudential reasons not to violate rights in order to avoid disaster, for example, when they would face legal sanctions and punishment, a proponent of Exceptionalism might characterize dirty hands leadership as supererogatory.

One reason that one may find Exceptionalism compelling in dirty hands scenarios is that citizens may have an interest in a moral division of labor, where leaders can play by different rules so that the rest of us don't have to. In addition to Walzer, Dennis Thompson also defends a form of Exceptionalism in some dirty hands cases. Thompson (1987) argues that citizens authorize their democratically elected leaders to violate rights in their name and on their behalf. On the other hand, insofar as Exceptionalism can enable leaders to act on citizens' preferences without requiring citizens to authorize rights violations explicitly, citizens may be able to keep their hands entirely clean. In this vein, David Archer (2013) argues that citizens are morally complicit when their democratically elected leaders violate moral requirements in their name during dirty hands situations. Or, as Hollis (1996) says, "When their hands get dirty, so do ours."[15]

Alternatively, one might favor Exceptionalism in dirty hands cases for pragmatic reasons. According to this view, leaders should be authorized to violate moral requirements to avoid disaster. Still, ordinary people should not because all members of the moral community have an interest in refraining from adopting rules that give too many people the authority to violate rights. Yet, this view is also difficult to defend on principled grounds because, presumably, any reason to respect a person's rights during ordinary times is also a reason to respect their rights when the numbers are against them, and there is the potential for disaster.[16] And any reason to violate rights for the sake of the greater good has equal force when the greater good falls short of a moral catastrophe.

Proponents of Exceptionalism in dirty hands cases rarely explain how leaders ought to discern the tipping point when a person's rights no longer carry weight against the moral significance of the greater good. But if there were some principles that could distinguish dirty hands situations from ordinary cases where the duty to respect rights conflicts with the moral reason to promote wellbeing, then anyone could follow that principle.[17] Leaders are not distinctively well placed to discern when the circumstances call for dirty hands, so even if dirty hands leadership were justified in some cases, this fact alone would not discredit the case for Consistency.

5. ROLE OBLIGATIONS

Another objection to Consistency is that it is seemingly at odds with the idea that leaders have distinctive permissions and obligations related to fiduciary duties or confidentiality requirements. In this section, I will address a few versions of this objection. The first version of the objection states that some leadership roles are intrinsically normatively distinctive in that they generate role obligations. The second version of the objection states that leadership is morally distinctive because leaders can have fiduciary duties that others lack. The third version of the objection states that leadership is morally distinctive because leaders have a distinctive legal status in many contexts. The fourth version of the objection states that leadership is distinctive because, as a cultural practice, people treat leaders differently.

Consider first the claim that some people in leadership roles have special role-based permissions and obligations that ordinary people lack (Hardimon, 1994). A proponent of Exceptionalism may appeal to this idea as a way of explaining how leaders also might be held to different moral standards. One example of a role obligation that seemingly grants people distinctive permissions and obligations in virtue of their role includes defense attorneys' obligations to defend guilty clients. Ordinarily, it would be wrong for anyone to help a guilty person get away with a crime. However, defense attorneys are permitted to assist criminals by virtue of their professional role. To take another example, people who occupy positions of religious authority cannot be compelled to testify or to violate clergy-penitent privilege. So too, an Exceptionalist might argue that different moral rules apply to leaders by virtue of their leadership role.

In response to this line of argument, a proponent of Consistency may reply that while Exceptionalism is justified in some cases, leadership isn't one of them. After all, so many people occupy leadership roles that it is unlikely that leadership per se licenses any presumptive exceptions to general moral obligations in the way that religious authority does, for example. Alternatively, a proponent of Consistency might maintain their rejection of Exceptionalism even for the aforementioned role obligations (Skerker, 2020). Michael Huemer (2016), for example, makes the case that defense attorneys should not defend clients that they know to be guilty. As for confidentiality permissions, what first appears to be a role-based exception to subpoenas that compel people to testify might actually reveal that no one has a duty to assist law enforcement in investigating and punishing criminals. Brian Barry (2000) once famously made an argument that is structurally similar to these responses regarding the value of liberal neutrality and religious exemptions. Barry argued that insofar as public officials have compelling reasons to grant exemptions from legal requirements for some groups, they should abolish those legal requirements for everyone. If a legal requirement should not be abolished for everyone, then it should be enforced without exceptions.

A Consistency theorist might also question whether the concept of role obligations is a useful way to understand the ethical challenges associated with particular roles. Insofar as leaders have distinctive permissions and obligations, they do not have this exceptional moral status by virtue of their role per se but rather by virtue of their circumstances. After all, different cultures conceive of roles in normatively different ways. For any given role, one could just provide an alternative conceptual analysis of the role that failed to include any morally distinctive exceptions (Cane, 2016).

Second, a proponent of Exceptionalism might defend their position by pointing out that leaders often have legal obligations, including fiduciary duties, which others lack (Renzo & Green, 2022). Fiduciary duties are legal or moral requirements that someone acts on another person's behalf. They can include duties of care, duties of loyalty, and heightened duties of honesty and disclosure.

People acquire fiduciary duties when they consent to a relationship that explicitly includes these duties. Yet, a proponent of Consistency needn't deny that some people have fiduciary duties to deny Exceptionalism. Rather, a proponent of Consistency will argue that everyone ought to honor the fiduciary duties that they voluntarily assume. The fact that leaders are more likely to have fiduciary duties to members of an organization or a community is a contingent feature of their circumstances. Still, it does not reveal that leadership is fundamentally morally distinctive.

Third, some philosophers argue that legal institutions can, to some extent, specify the boundaries of people's moral obligations and entitlements.[18] An Exceptionalist who held this view may then point out that leaders often have an exceptional legal status. For example, public officials have the legal authority to coerce and incarcerate people. Public officials are given immunity from criminal prosecution associated with their professional roles.[19] In private contexts, leaders are sometimes held to heightened legal liability standards. For example, unlike most workers, corporate executives are legally required to implement policies that promote the long-term market value of their firms.[20]

Consistency theorists should deny the premise that the content of people's moral obligations and entitlements depend in any way on whether they are entrenched in law. But even granting this premise, a proponent of Consistency can reply in two ways. First, a proponent of Consistency might argue that the law shouldn't grant leaders special permissions, obligations, and immunities. After all, it is generally a desideratum of legal frameworks that they do not make special exceptions for certain groups of people, and that desideratum should extend to public and industry leaders.[21] Or, a proponent of Consistency could argue that even if leaders acquire some distinctive permissions and obligations under some legal systems, the same more general moral requirements that apply to everyone else continue to apply to leaders as well. On this view, leadership may be morally distinctive, but leaders are still bound by their more general moral obligations, which apply to everyone with equal normative force.

6. IMPLICATIONS FOR DEVELOPMENT

So far, I have described the distinction between Exceptionalism and Consistency, and I made a tentative case for Consistency as an approach to leadership ethics. In this section, I discuss the implications of Consistency for the study and teaching of ethical leadership. I argue that there are serious risks to approaching leadership in a way that implicitly assumes that it is morally distinctive. Instead, leadership scholarship and development should emphasize that leaders are people, too, and they ought to be held to the same standards of permission, obligation, praise, and blame as the rest of us.

The top-line practical implication of the foregoing argument is that leaders, leadership scholars, and educators should rethink any implicit or explicit endorsement of Exceptionalism. In this chapter, I mainly argue that Exceptionalism is an implausible moral theory because the landscape of moral permissions and obligations should hold everyone to the same standards.[22] But even if one is unconvinced by this argument, promoting Exceptionalism to leaders is morally risky because leaders may be tempted to appeal to Exceptionalism as a way of avoiding accountability altogether. Even if many people in organizations, including leaders, believe that people in formal positions of authority should be held to different moral standards than others in the organization, these perceptions of ethics are not a reliable guide to ethical decision-making. One reason to be skeptical of the narrative of leaders' exceptional status is so often self-serving for the leaders who espouse it. If Consistency were the norm in leadership ethics, then leaders would be required to justify their conduct to stakeholders without an appeal to their professional position or role. Followers could hold leaders accountable by applying everyday moral requirements to those who have power over them.[23]

There are also compelling egalitarian reasons for leaders, leadership scholars, and educators to endorse Consistency in leadership ethics. Consistency can explain why hypocritical leadership is so objectionable. As the philosopher Jay Wallace (2010) has argued, hypocrisy is wrong because people who hypocritically blame others for things that they also do are holding other people to moral standards that they are unwilling to apply to themselves. By exempting themselves from standards of blame, hypocrites deny that they are morally equal to the people they blame and judge. Leaders who subscribe to an ethic of Exceptionalism are hypocritical in this sense.

One may reply that leaders who endorse Exceptionalism often hold themselves to more demanding moral standards and do not exempt themselves from the standards of blame that they apply to other people.[24] I grant that Exceptionalism could subject leaders to heightened moral standards – more scrutiny and more opportunities for blame. But even this morally ambitious form of Exceptionalism denies the moral equality between leaders and followers. When leaders hold themselves to ambitious moral requirements but do not apply them to others, they endorse the condescending view that other people should be subject to lower moral expectations.[25] This version of Exceptionalism also, therefore, expresses a disrespectful attitude about non-leaders moral capacities.

Relatedly, Consistency in leadership ethics might require that followers take more responsibility for their actions than Exceptionalism. Though leaders may appeal to Exceptionalism to avoid being held accountable by the standards of interpersonal morality, followers may also appeal to Exceptionalism to avoid being held accountable for what they do as members of an organization. Returning to the analogy to just war theory, proponents of the orthodox view sometimes argue that enlisted soldiers should not deliberate about whether they are fighting for a just cause.[26] At the same time, orthodox theorists also argue that officers and public officials should not be held legally responsible for starting or participating in an unjust war.[27] This view, therefore, creates a situation where no one can be held accountable for killing in the service of an unjust cause.

More generally, the belief in Exceptionalism may create responsibility voids in other organizations too (Duijf, 2018). If different rules apply to leaders, and followers are not responsible for what they do on behalf of their leaders, then to whom can the victims of bad leadership appeal to when followers violate common sense interpersonal moral requirements? Consider, for example, how some policies require citizens to comply with unjust laws and also leaders from being held personally liable for passing and enforcing the law. In these cases, the victims of unjust law enforcement have no recourse in pressing claims for compensation or in advocating for an apology.

The case for Consistency potentially has revisionary implications for leadership ethics instruction and leadership development. Instead of studying distinctive principles and guidelines for leaders, leaders should learn about the same principles in moral philosophy that apply to all other decision-makers. Similarly, leaders should invest in developing general all-purpose abilities, such as interpersonal communication skills and critical thinking, which will serve them well in helping them to comply with their moral obligations to avoid deception and to hold themselves to the same moral standards that apply to their coworkers and other stakeholders.

7. CONCLUSION

Taking stock, in this chapter, I argued against Exceptionalism and favoring Consistency in leadership scholarship, education, and development. I first made the case that many leaders, scholars, and educators implicitly endorse Exceptionalism. There, I drew an analogy between Exceptionalism and just war theory and theories of political obligation.

I then argued against Exceptionalism and in favor of Consistency, further drawing on work from these analogous debates in political philosophy. Next, I considered and replied to two objections – dirty hands and role obligations. In response to this line of argument, some readers may instead find that the intuitive price of accepting Consistency is too high, and they may then read the foregoing discussion of dirty hands and role obligation cases as a reduction of the Consistency approach. I cannot rule out this possibility, but the arguments for Consistency in the context of dirty hands and role obligation cases show that Consistency needn't be as revisionary as it may initially seem and that even if Exceptionalism provides a justification for leaders' actual conduct, people who defend Exceptionalism in these cases are committed to a more revisionary general ethical theory, compared to Consistency theorists.

I concluded that people should be more skeptical of theories and approaches that implicitly endorse Exceptionalism in leadership ethics. My case for Consistency also makes a methodological point about leadership ethics by showing that leadership theorists cannot assume that the fact that someone occupies a position of power or authority is normatively significant. Scholars who study leadership have long debated the meaning of the term "leadership" as if conceptual analysis could settle normative debates about leaders' rights and obligations. Yet, this approach is misguided because the folk concept of "leadership" can refer to many kinds of relationships, and any revisionary analysis of "leadership" that yielded specific conclusions about leadership ethics would, therefore, require characterizing leadership in a way that already took a stand on questions about leadership ethics (Ciulla, 2020). Leadership scholars cannot conclude that leadership is morally distinctive simply by defining the concept in a moralized way. Rather, questions about whether *Consistency* or *Exceptionalism* is the better approach to leadership ethics must be settled through philosophical argument and consideration of the moral reasons that apply to leaders.

NOTES

1. At the farthest end of this extreme, some Exceptionalists may believe that moral requirements simply don't apply to leaders. This position is consistent with some readings of Machiavelli or Nietzsche. The finding that leaders are more likely to display "dark triad" personality traits may also reveal that people who are indifferent to moral norms are over-represented in leadership positions. For the sake of clarity, I do not consider this version of Exceptionalism in my analysis.
2. For example, prominent theories of leadership including transformative leadership and servant leadership propose that leaders hold themselves to ethical standards that are distinct from others in the organization. For an overview of research on these two leadership styles, see Gregory Stone et al. (2004).
3. See, for example, the Center for Creative Leadership, a leader-centric research, development, and consulting firm.
4. See, for example, the Multifactor Leadership Questionnaire, which evaluates leaders in terms of the extent that they have a transformational leadership style (Batista-Foguet et al., 2021).
5. Burns' (1978) work on the subject is a good example of this trend.
6. For an overview, see Lazar (2017).
7. Sometimes this is characterized in terms of feasibility constraints on ethical theories of just conduct in war (Lazar & Valentini, 2017).
8. For a discussion of the underlying methodological disputes that explain the orthodox/revisionist divide, see Lazar and Valentini (2017).
9. See, for example, O'Connor and Kearney (2023) and Wang (2020).
10. For an overview of this debate, see Huemer and Layman (2021).
11. For an overview of this debate, see Lazar (2020).
12. Russ Shafer-Landau (2020) makes this point along with other arguments in defense of moral objectivity.
13. Joanne Ciulla (2003) makes this point in her work.
14. In contrast, some realist theorists of international relations deny this claim, for example, Morgenthau et al. (2005).
15. As cited in Coady (2024).
16. For defenses of a view like this, see Anscombe (2022) and Taurek (1977).
17. I take it that this is Nozick's view in discussions of whether entitlements may be violated to avoid catastrophic moral horror (Nozick, 1974).
18. For an extended account of how this may be a justifiable approach to political leadership, see Pallikkathayil (2010).
19. Though this practice is controversial, see Schwartz (2017).
20. The business judgment rule is one example of this, see Sharfman (2017).
21. This principle is sometimes called legal egalitarianism. It requires that all people subject to the law have equal legal protections, including the same formal legal rights and rights of due process for everyone.
22. I elaborate on this argument elsewhere (Flanigan, 2018).
23. Accountability is especially important in organizations where leaders can use their power in self-serving ways that are harmful to the institution (Rus et al., 2012).
24. For example, leadership theorists who emphasize the importance of leading as a moral exemplar may press this line in response to the argument.

25. Joanne Ciulla (2003) makes this point as well.
26. For an overview of this debate, see the symposium on Jeff McMahan's (2013) work in the *Boston Review*.
27. Some revisionist Just War theorists also argue that unjust combatants and officials should not be punished, but they depart from orthodox theorists in nevertheless maintaining that unjust combatants and officials are liable to be punished. Revisionists oppose punishment for pragmatic reasons, whereas orthodox theorists who endorse the principle of the moral equality of combatants oppose punishment because they have an Exceptionalist moral theory. For various accounts of unjust combatants' and officials' legal liability to be punished, see Rodin and Shue (2010).

REFERENCES

Anscombe, G. E. M. (2022). Who is wronged? (A reply to Philippa Foot). In D. R. DeNicola (Ed.), *A reader in moral philosophy* (p. 24), Broadview Press.
Archer, D. (2013, August). Dirty hands and the complicity of the democratic public. *Ethical Theory and Moral Practice*, *16*(4), 777–790. https://doi.org/10.1007/s10677-012-9387-y
Barry, B. (2000). *Culture and equality: An egalitarian critique of multiculturalism* (1st ed.). Polity.
Batista-Foguet, J. M., Esteve, M., & van Witteloostuijn, A. (2021, July 22). Measuring leadership an assessment of the multifactor leadership questionnaire. *PLOS ONE*, *16*(7), e0254329. https://doi.org/10.1371/journal.pone.0254329
Brännmark, J. (2016). Moral disunitarianism. *The Philosophical Quarterly (1950-)*, *66*(264), 481–499.
Burns, J. M. (1978). *Leadership* (1st ed.). HarperCollins.
Cane, P. (2016). Role responsibility. *The Journal of Ethics*, *20*(1–3), 279–298.
Christiano, T. (2004). The authority of democracy. *Journal of Political Philosophy*, *12*(3), 266–290. https://doi.org/10.1111/j.1467-9760.2004.00200.x
Ciulla, J. B. (2003). *[Introduction to] The ethics of leadership*. Wadsworth/Thomson Learning.
Ciulla, J. B. (2020). Ethics and effectiveness: The nature of good leadership. In *The search for ethics in leadership, business, and beyond* (Issues in Business Ethics, Vol. 50, pp. 3–32). Springer International Publishing. https://doi.org/10.1007/978-3-030-38463-0_1
Coady, C. A. J. (2024, Spring). The problem of dirty hands. In E. N. Zalta & U. Nodelman (Eds.), *The Stanford encyclopedia of philosophy*. Metaphysics Research Lab, Stanford University. https://plato.stanford.edu/archives/spr2024/entries/dirty-hands/
Duijf, H. (2018, July 1). Responsibility voids and cooperation. *Philosophy of the Social Sciences*, *48*(4), 434–460. https://doi.org/10.1177/0048393118767084
Flanigan, J. (2018). Duty and enforcement. *Journal of Political Philosophy*, *27*(3), 341–362. https://doi.org/10.1111/jopp.12173
Ford, S. B. (2022, October 2). Moral exceptionalism and the just war tradition: Walzer's instrumentalist approach and an institutionalist response to McMahan's 'Nazi military' problem. *Journal of Military Ethics*, *21*(3–4), 210–227. https://doi.org/10.1080/15027570.2022.2156062
Goodin, R. E. (1995). *Utilitarianism as a public philosophy* (Cambridge Studies in Philosophy and Public Policy). Cambridge University Press. https://doi.org/10.1017/CBO9780511625053
Gregory Stone, A., Russell, R. F., & Patterson, K. (2004, January 1). Transformational versus servant leadership: A difference in leader focus. *Leadership & Organization Development Journal*, *25*(4), 349–361. https://doi.org/10.1108/01437730410538671
Hardimon, M. O. (1994). Role obligations. *The Journal of Philosophy*, *91*(7), 333–363. https://doi.org/10.2307/2940934
Hollis, M. (1996). *Reason in action: Essays in the philosophy of social science*. Cambridge University Press.
Huemer, M. (2013). *The problem of political authority: An examination of the right to coerce and the duty to obey* (1st ed.). Palgrave Macmillan.
Huemer, M. (2016). Devil's advocates: On the ethics of unjust legal advocacy. In E. Crookston, D. Killoren, & J. Trerise (Eds.), *Ethics in politics: The rights and obligations of individual political agents* (pp. 295–314). Routledge.
Huemer, M., & Layman, D. (2021). *Is political authority an illusion?: A debate*. Routledge.

Jay Wallace, R. (2010). Hypocrisy, moral address, and the equal standing of persons. *Philosophy & Public Affairs, 38*(4), 307–341.
John Simmons, A. (1999). Justification and legitimacy. *Ethics, 109*(4), 739–771. https://doi.org/10.1086/233944
Klosko, G. (1987). Presumptive benefit, fairness, and political obligation. *Philosophy & Public Affairs, 16*(3), 241–259.
Lazar, S. (2013). Associative duties and the ethics of killing in war. *Journal of Practical Ethics, 1*(1), 3–48. https://papers.ssrn.com/sol3/papers.cfm?abstract_id=2463212
Lazar, S. (2017). Just war theory: Revisionists vs traditionalists. *Annual Review of Political Science, 20*, 37–54.
Lazar, S. (2020, Spring). War. In E. N. Zalta (Ed.), *The Stanford encyclopedia of philosophy*. Metaphysics Research Lab, Stanford University. https://plato.stanford.edu/archives/spr2020/entries/war/
Lazar, S., & Valentini, L. (2017). Proxy battles in just war theory: Jus in Bello, the site of justice, and feasibility constraints. In D. Sobel, P. Vallentyne, & S. Wall (Eds.), *Oxford studies in political philosophy*: Volume 3 (pp. 166–193). Oxford University Press.
McMahan, J. (2004). The ethics of killing in war. *Ethics, 114*(4), 693–733. https://doi.org/10.1086/422400
McMahan, J. (2009). *Killing in war*. Oxford University Press. https://doi.org/10.1093/acprof:oso/9780199548668.001.0001
McMahan, J. (2013, October 28). The moral responsibility of volunteer soldiers. *Boston Review*. https://www.bostonreview.net/forum/moral-wounds-ethics-volunteer-military-service/
Morgenthau, H., Thompson, K., & Clinton, D. (2005). *Politics among nations* (7th ed.). McGraw-Hill Education.
Nozick, R. (1974). *Anarchy, state, and utopia* (Vol. 5038, p. 30). Basic Books.
O'Connor, F. G., & Kearney, F. H. (2023). Leadership lessons learned from the military. *Clinics in Sports Medicine, 42*(2), 301–315.
Pallikkathayil, J. (2010, October). Deriving morality from politics: Rethinking the formula of humanity. *Ethics, 121*(1), 116–147. https://doi.org/10.1086/656041
Price, T. L. (2000). Explaining ethical failures of leadership. *Leadership & Organization Development Journal, 21*(4), 177–184.
Rawls, J. (2005). *Political liberalism* (Expanded ed.). Columbia University Press.
Renzo, M., & Green, L. (2022). Legal obligation and authority. In E. N. Zalta & U. Nodelman (Eds.), *The Stanford encyclopedia of philosophy*. Metaphysics Research Lab, Stanford University. https://plato.stanford.edu/archives/fall2022/entries/legal-obligation/
Rodin, D., & Shue, H. (2010). *Just and unjust warriors: The moral and legal status of soldiers*. Oxford University Press.
Rus, D., van Knippenberg, D., & Wisse, B. (2012, February 1). Leader power and self-serving behavior: The moderating role of accountability. *The Leadership Quarterly, 23*(1), 13–26. https://doi.org/10.1016/j.leaqua.2011.11.002
Scheffler, S. (1997). Relationships and responsibilities. *Philosophy & Public Affairs, 26*(3), 189–209.
Schwartz, J. C. (2017). How qualified immunity fails. *The Yale Law Journal, 127*(1), 2–76.
Shafer-Landau, R. (2020). *The fundamentals of ethics* (5th ed.). Oxford University Press.
Sharfman, B. S. (2017). The importance of the business judgment rule. *New York University Journal of Law and Business, 14*(1), 27–70.
Skerker, M. (2020). Individual responsibility for collective action. In *The Routledge handbook of collective responsibility*. Routledge.
Taurek, J. M. (1977). Should the numbers count. *Philosophy & Public Affairs, 6*(4), 293–316.
Thompson, D. (1987). *Political ethics and public office* (1st ed.). Harvard University Press.
Waldron, J. (2005). Torture and positive law: Jurisprudence for the White House. *Columbia Law Review, 105*, 1681.
Walzer, M. (2015). *Just and unjust wars* (5th ed.). Basic Books.
Wang, F. (2020, January 1). Social justice leadership and *The Art of War*. *Critical Studies in Education, 61*(1), 86–100. https://doi.org/10.1080/17508487.2017.1327877

CHAPTER 5

DEFENDING THE LIVES OF OTHERS: A DUTY TO FORCEFULLY INTERVENE?

Shannon Brandt Ford

International Relations, Curtin University, Perth, Australia

ABSTRACT

Responsibility to Protect (R2P) doctrine assumes that there exists an underlying humanitarian duty to forcefully intervene in situations where innocent human lives are threatened with unjust violence. But what is the philosophical basis for the humanitarian moral obligation that underpins the R2P doctrine? I demonstrate that a third party should use forceful intervention (which might include lethal force) to protect an innocent human life in cases where the intervener has a duty to rescue the potential victim's life and the use of force is morally permissible. Then I argue that a potential intervener is permitted to kill the attacker when he has an impartial reason for doing so: the attacker is unjustly threatening an innocent person's life. Impartial justification is important in such cases, I argue, because it affirms the equality of all humans: that one human is not worth intrinsically more than another.

Keywords: Self-defence; defence of others; Responsibility to Protect; duty to rescue; intervention

INTRODUCTION

The last two decades have witnessed the emergence of a norm that supports military intervention to protect people whose lives are unjustly threatened: the purported 'Responsibility to Protect' (R2P) doctrine. The R2P literature is concerned with the obligation of states to protect the lives of vulnerable people, including people outside a state's own jurisdiction (Bellamy, 2014; Chesterman, 2011; Dobos, 2011; Doyle, 2011; Finnemore, 1996; Kuperman, 2013; Pattison, 2010; Weiss, 2012; Wheeler, 2000). In other words, it promotes the idea that one state (or a coalition of states) should, in some cases, militarily intervene in the domestic affairs of other states to rescue groups of people whose lives are unjustly threatened. In the introduction to a special edition of *Ethics and International Affairs* devoted to R2P, Michael Ignatieff (2021) suggested that the world has changed since the International Commission on Intervention and State Sovereignty published the report that came to be known as *The Responsibility to Protect* in 2001. He argues that it is no longer the right time to push for the adoption of R2P norms because 'the whole project belongs to a vanished era' of American ascendancy (Ignatieff, 2021, p. 178). At the same time, however, he reiterated his belief in the ultimate value of the R2P doctrine.

> Good ideas do not always die just because the times in which they were first articulated turn out to be too barren for them to sprout. They remain on the ground, seeds awaiting a time to germinate. (Ignatieff, 2021, p. 179)

In the spirit of creating one of these seeds to germinate, here I consider what we can learn about the R2P at the level of individuals. In other words, what is the philosophical basis for the humanitarian moral obligation that underpins the R2P doctrine? Mark Bevir and Ian Hall (2020) make the case for examining such underlying philosophical positions. They suggest that clear philosophy enhances the sharpness and clarity of individual research (Bevir & Hall, 2020, p. 123). In our case, there is a small but significant discussion within the philosophical literature in relation to defence of others that might be considered when thinking about R2P. Cecile Fabre (2007), in particular, makes a convincing argument defending a humanitarian duty of forceful intervention – what she describes as mandatory rescue killings. She argues that the duty to provide assistance includes a duty to help others ward off attackers, by exercising lethal force if necessary (Fabre, 2007, p. 364). Fabre points out that the question of 'whether or not individuals are under a duty to kill in defence of another is of enormous moral, political and legal importance'. The implication being, she believes, that powerful states are therefore under a moral obligation to wage a war of intervention in defence of a genocidal tyrant's victims (Fabre, 2007, p. 363).

In this chapter, I similarly defend an argument for a humanitarian duty to forcefully intervene in cases where an innocent human life is threatened with unjust violence. I argue that a third party should use forceful intervention (which might include lethal force) to protect an innocent human life in cases where the intervener has a duty to rescue the potential victim's life and the use of force is morally permissible. To say that the use of force is morally permissible means that a potential victim has a right to be protected from an unjust threat. Ultimately, we should intervene when we are capable of doing so, it is necessary to prevent the wrongful death of an innocent human, and it is not unreasonably risky or costly.

But then in the second section, I argue, contra Fabre, that morally justified forceful intervention should primarily be based on impartial reasons. Fabre argues that individuals are entitled to confer greater weight to their own interests, and this is the basis for their right to defend themselves against a culpable attacker. She then suggests that a potential victim has the power to confer this permission to kill the attacker on a potential rescuer (Fabre, 2009, p. 163). In contrast, I argue that a potential intervener is permitted to kill the attacker because he has an impartial reason for doing so: the attacker is unjustly threatening an innocent person's life. All other things being equal, a third party must satisfy the same impartial moral requirements that hold for self-defence. Impartial justification is important in such cases, I argue, because it affirms the equality of all humans: that one human is not worth intrinsically more than another.

A HUMANITARIAN DUTY TO FORCEFULLY INTERVENE

Intrinsically Valuable Lives

I start with the presumption that human lives are morally valuable and this makes them worth defending. Or, to put it another way, the life of a human being is something that is *intrinsically valuable*. According to Ronald Dworkin (1993, p. 71), something is intrinsically valuable if 'its value is independent of what people happen to enjoy or want or need or what is good for them'. In contrast, he suggests, something is instrumentally valuable if its value depends on its usefulness in getting something else they want. If we hold the view that human life is intrinsically valuable, then it is a very morally weighty consideration in our decision-making. In other words, it doesn't become less valuable under certain circumstances. John Locke (1988 [1689], pp. 278–279), for instance, suggests that the protection of innocent human lives should be made a priority in situations of mortal danger, 'For by the Fundamental Law of Nature, Man being to be preserved, as much as possible, when all cannot be preserv'd, the safety of the Innocent is to be preferred'. Some might dispute the presumption that human life has intrinsic value, however. What property of a human life, after all, gives it intrinsic value when compared to other forms of life?[1] I rely on the accounts of rights theorists such as James Griffin (2008, pp. 33–37) who suggests that a human being is intrinsically valuable because personhood is valuable; what he describes as a 'substantive' account of personhood.[2] The key point of a substantive account of personhood, such as Griffin's, is that human life is qualitatively 'different from the life of other animals'.[3] Human life is valuable because it is 'human' life.

> We human beings have a conception of ourselves and of our past and future. We reflect and assess. We form pictures of what a good life would be .... And we try to realize these pictures. This is what we mean by a distinctly human existence. (Griffin, 2008, p. 33)

Griffin (2008) says that we 'value our status as human beings especially highly' and that human rights should be seen as 'protections of our human standing or ... our personhood' (p. 33). To say that a human has intrinsic value then is to make it a primary moral end. That is, it is the main goal of protection rather than the means to secure other rights.

Having stipulated that the intrinsic value of human lives is our starting assumption, I now suggest that this translates into a general humanitarian duty to rescue human lives in danger. That is, we all have an obligation to intervene and rescue a human whose life is in danger. Imagine a situation where a child is swimming at the beach, and he has been struck by an unusually big wave so that he is now panicking and struggling to stay afloat. You happen to be taking a stroll along the shallows when you notice the stricken child, and you quickly recognise you are the only person who can get to him in time before the next wave strikes. Without your immediate help, he will almost certainly drown. Since you are an experienced beachgoer and good swimmer, the risk to you is insignificant. But your brand new iPhone is in your pocket and it will be wrecked if you dive into the waves to save the child. We should agree that in such a situation we all have a duty to rescue the child when the risk and cost to us is so comparably insignificant. Peter Singer (1972, pp. 231–232) describes this humanitarian 'duty to rescue' in the following way:

> If it is in our power to prevent something bad from happening, without thereby sacrificing anything morally significant, we ought, morally, to do it. An application of this principle would be as follows: if I am walking past a shallow pond and see a child drowning in it, I ought to wade in and pull the child out. This will mean getting my clothes muddy, but this is insignificant, while the death of the child would presumably be a very bad thing.

Both these hypothetical cases highlight a number of considerations in relation to a humanitarian duty to rescue. First, in a case where a human's life is threatened, but can be preserved by the intervention of another person, then choosing to rescue a life is clearly a morally good choice. Protecting the life of a child who is about to drown is a better outcome than letting him die, all other things being equal. Additionally, a capable person should intervene if the child is dependent on the capable person to save his life. We might imagine that we are the only person on the scene who can save the child. As Scott James (2007, p. 238) points out, we should rescue a human who is uniquely dependent on us to intervene; that is, an individual who relies on you and only you for help. If we are the only person who is in a position to save the child, then we have a moral responsibility to intervene because the child is depending upon us alone for his life. Nobody else can save the child.

But what if the potential intervener cannot swim? He might be putting his own life in serious jeopardy by attempting to save the child. If the potential intervener was likely to die or be seriously injured, then the attempt to rescue the child would be a supererogatory act (and/or possibly foolish). This does not then mean that the potential intervener's duty to rescue has disappeared, however. The intervener should still seek other means to rescue the child, such as calling for help or throwing the child a rope. A capable person should personally intervene to rescue the child's life if it is not significantly costly or risky to him. After all, it would be a callous person who would allow a child to drown because he did not want to wreck his iPhone. In short, a capable person is morally obliged to rescue an innocent person's life if it is not unreasonably costly or risky to the rescuer. This is especially the case if we are the only person who is in a position to intervene and rescue the innocent person.

A Duty to Forcefully Intervene

One might agree that we all have an obligation to rescue another human when faced with a situation meeting the conditions required for an act of rescue listed above, but then object if it requires him to deliberately harm another human, particularly when the act of rescue is likely to be lethal. Is there still a duty to rescue (in order to protect a human life) when it is necessary to forcefully intervene? I argue that the humanitarian duty to rescue humans from being killed can include the use of forceful intervention. Let us imagine a situation similar to the one described above, where a child is close to drowning, and you are the only person who can intervene to save the child's life. But in this particular case, the source of the threat to the child's life is an adult who is deliberately holding the child under the water. You yell at the murderous adult to stop but he ignores you. The only way to rescue the innocent child is to use physical force to stop the actions of the murderous adult. If the level of force necessary to save the child is minimal, such as physically restraining the adult or pushing him over, then I suspect those of us who agreed to the principle of a duty to rescue (as outlined above) would have no problem agreeing to its application here. It is difficult to see how it would not apply since any harm to the adult is likely to be incidental and very minor in comparison to the child's death. Furthermore, we should also agree to more serious uses of forceful intervention that are non-lethal. If we agree that minimal harm to the murderous adult is justifiable when it is necessary to save the child's life, then we should agree to more serious harms – such as breaking the adult's arm or giving him concussion – if this saves the child's life. After all, the harm we are doing to the adult by using forceful intervention is well short of the harm the adult is inflicting upon the child. If this is correct, then this means that we have a duty to use some degree of forceful intervention if it is necessary to save the child's life.

But should the duty to rescue still apply in cases where it is necessary to use lethal force to save the child's life or where there is a significant risk that our intervention will kill the murderous adult? In other words, do we have a duty to kill the murderous adult if that is the only reasonable way to save the child's life? I argue that we do. We know that unjust killing is a serious moral wrong and killing a human is to destroy something that is of great moral value. The lives of both the murderous adult and the child are morally valuable and should be preserved, if at all possible. But in this case, the adult is unjustly threatening the child's life. As we'll see in the section below, this means that the murderous adult does not have the same protection as the innocent child. If we agree that we have a duty to rescue the child, then it seems plausible to suggest that, in combination with the permissibility of killing the adult, we are duty-bound to forcefully intervene by killing the adult, if that is the level of force necessary to save the child.

There is a particular purpose in emphasising a humanitarian duty to forcefully intervene to rescue innocent humans from being killed. George Fletcher (1990, p. 175) suggests that there is little need to constrain our natural impulses with an imperative to save ourselves. As Locke (1988 [1689], p. 206) argues in reference to self-preservation:

> The first and strongest desire God Planted in Men, and wrought into the very Principles of their Nature being that of Self-preservation, that is the Foundation of a right to the Creatures, for the particular support and use of each individual Person himself.

But, we do, sometimes, need to be reminded of our obligation to rescue others. In cases where there is little cost or risk for us, it might be clear that we should intervene to save the life of an innocent human. But this becomes less clear when the intervention is costly or risky. Think again of the original case of the child who is drowning and needs us to rescue him. We should rescue someone who is dependent upon our intervention. But what if there is a shark in the water or a storm has whipped up the surf so that the waves are extremely hazardous? Are we obliged to accept high levels of cost and risk to ourselves in order to save others? And if so, where do we draw the line on the amount of sacrifice we are obliged to make for the lives of others? According to Fletcher (1990, p. 176), thinking about defensive intervention as a duty-based act of rescue seems to threaten the universality of the right to defend others. After all, he asks, is one under a duty to rescue everyone?

Any situation requiring forceful intervention is likely to be risky, particularly when lethal force is necessary.[4] The most obvious source of danger to us in forcefully intervening is from the attacker (whom we are using force against), if he chooses to fight back. In addition, a forceful intervener has two other sources of risk and cost to consider. There could be other interveners who might choose, for whatever reason, to side with the attacker. The intervener might end up having to deal with a number of attackers. Furthermore, a forceful intervener is likely to face serious consequences for killing or injuring the attacker. If the intervener makes a mistake, and wrongfully kills an innocent human, then he is likely to face criminal charges. If eventually acquitted, the experience of being taken to court to face a serious criminal charge (especially unlawful killing or murder) is still likely to be harrowing, and it might drag on for years. And even if the intervener proves to be justified in his actions, he still must live with the psychological and emotional burden of killing another human being. He might also be the subject of retaliation if the family or friends of the attacker seek revenge.

In short, the obligation to forcefully intervene is weakened for the average person, when the intervention is risky and/or costly. The riskier and costlier the intervention, the weaker the obligation to rescue. Although the humanitarian duty to forcefully intervene continues to exist, we should expect that most situations requiring the use of deadly force will be risky and/or costly. This helps explain why some people might believe that intervention using lethal force is not an obligation. If the only way I could save the innocent child from being drowned was to risk my own life by attacking the murderous adult, then I suspect many people would consider it a supererogatory act rather than something one is duty-bound to do. In contrast, it is more difficult to object to rescuing a life that requires little or no sacrifice on our part.

IMPARTIAL MORAL JUSTIFICATION
Fabre's Partiality Account

Up to this point, my argument largely coheres with Fabre's account for defence of others. We both agree that there can be a duty to kill an unjust attacker in cases where it is necessary to rescue an innocent human life, and that the risk and/or cost to the potential intervener plays a key role in the applicability of this obligation (Fabre, 2007, p. 366). But here is where our accounts come apart. Unlike Fabre, I argue that a third-party intervener is morally *permitted* to use lethal force against an unjust threat with reasons that satisfy the same *impartial* moral requirements that hold for killing in self-defence. Consider the following hypothetical case. Meg tries to shoot Sam in order to kill him and take his wallet. But Dean is standing nearby and he can see that Meg is about to shoot Sam. Dean is quicker on the draw than Meg and intervenes by shooting her first and thus saves Sam's life. In this case, the intervener (Dean) acts on behalf of the victim (Sam) to prevent him from being killed by the attacker (Meg). All other things being equal, Dean is morally justified in killing Meg in order to rescue Sam.

When a third-party intervenes (Dean) to defend the victim of a deadly attack (Sam), the intervener's action is morally justified by the victim's possession of the right not to be killed. In other words, Sam's right not to be killed exists independently of personal preferences or interests. The use of third-party lethal force must be morally justified from this impartial standpoint, which holds for *any* reasonable observer. Such impartiality demands a disinterested approach to the facts of any situation. In contrast, Fabre's (2009) partialist approach to permissible rescue killings says that Sam has a vested interest in killing Meg, which others lack (p. 154). And that Sam's interest in surviving Meg's attack can be transferred as a right to Dean (Fabre, 2009, p. 158). Thomas Nagel (1991, p. 4) describes the distinction between impartialism and partialism in the following way:

> The impersonal standpoint in each of us produces ... a powerful demand for universal impartiality and equality, while the personal standpoint gives rise to individualistic motives and requirements which present obstacles to the pursuit and realisation of such ideals.

An impartial justification for the use of lethal force is important because it establishes the equality of all humans: that one human is *not* worth intrinsically more than another human. A third party should not base the use of lethal force on a personal preference for one person over against another because one human life is not intrinsically morally worthwhile than another. Hence, we should consider only impartial moral reasons as valid when an intervener is deciding whether to give preference to the life of a victim over an attacker.

Many moral justifications for killing in defence of others rely on impartiality to permit the intervener to choose the life of the victim over the life of the threat.

Judith Jarvis Thomson's account, for example, is impartial because she argues it is the fact that an unjust threat will otherwise kill a victim that justifies both killing in self-defence and killing in defence of others. According to Thomson (1991), the permissibility of a defender killing an unjust threat in self-defence goes hand-in-hand with the permissibility of an intervener killing an unjust threat to save the life of a victim (p. 306). Her account of morally justified killing in self-defence shares a common moral ground with her account of killing in defence of others. Moreover, because they derive moral justification from the same source, it is true to say that it is morally impermissible for an unjust threat to fight back in both situations (Thomson, 1991, p. 306). What this means, according to Thomson, is that it is not because of the personal interest in preserving his own life that a defender is justified in killing an unjust threat in self-defence. Rather, it is because of the disinterested fact that an unjust threat will otherwise violate a defender's right not to be killed that a defender may proceed in killing an unjust threat. And this impartial moral ground is the basis for forceful intervention by a third party (Thomson, 1991, p. 308).

In a similar vein, Jeff McMahan argues for an approach to morally justified killing in self-defence that is based on the impartial principle of moral liability. According to McMahan (2005), a person who acts with justification to threaten another with harm, to which the other is morally liable, does not threaten to wrong that other person (p. 400). He suggests that 'it is not implausible to suppose that third parties must not intervene' in cases during war where neither innocent civilians nor the just combatants who threaten them are all equally non-liable to be killed. This is because, according to McMahan (2009), there must be an impartial reason to justify the intentional killing of non-liable persons for a third party to intervene on one side or the other (p. 49). Michael Gorr (1990) also puts forward an argument for an impartial principle that determines when it is morally permissible to inflict lethal harm on another human in order to protect oneself or some innocent third party. He refers to this moral principle as 'private defense'. Gorr's intent was to specify the necessary and sufficient conditions for the justifiable infliction of serious harm upon another human that can be applied equally well in either cases of self-defence or defence of others. He argues that,

> proportional defensive measures are warranted against any person who lacks justification for causing an otherwise unavoidable threat to the interests of another, regardless of whether or not that person is in any obvious sense an 'aggressor' and even whether or not she is culpable in bringing about such a situation. (Gorr, 1990, p. 241)

In short, the moral permissibility of killing in self-defence and killing in defence of others both have a common moral source. This is the impartial fact that the unjust threat will kill (or seriously injure) the victim/defender unless lethal force is used against the unjust threat.

Mere Self-preservationism?

My concern with Fabre's partiality account is that it does not satisfactorily maintain a clear distinction between permissible killing in self-defence and mere self-preservationism. According to Fabre (2009), one is permitted intentionally to kill in self-defence (on grounds of partiality) *if and only if* the following two conditions are met: (a) one's survival is at stake (*the necessity condition*); and (b) one is directly threatened by the target of one's self-defensive actions (*the egoist condition*) (p. 153). This is too similar to a self-preservationist (or Hobbesian) view that says that a person is *always* justified in using lethal force if it is necessary to preserve her life. Sharing common ground with the political realist, self-preservationism is a belief based in the notion that survival is the only human interest that matters. Hobbes (1996 [1651], p. 91) states that:

> The Right of Nature ... is the Liberty each man hath, to use his own power, as he will himself, for the preservation of his own Nature; that is to say, of his own Life; and consequently, of doing any thing, which in his own Judgement, and Reason, he shall conceive to be the aptest means thereunto

According to Bernard Gert (1967), this view – the rational avoidance of death – plays a central role in Hobbes's political theory. Hobbes held that self-defence is an inalienable right, which is grounded in one's rational concern with his own self-preservation (Gert, 1967, p. 518).

As an action, self-preservation is not necessarily a bad thing. Jenny Teichman (1986, p. 84) describes self-preservation as an act (or set of actions) intended to prevent or reduce harm to a person from a deadly threat. Acts of self-defence, she suggest, are an important subset of self-preservation in the sense they are 'those acts of self-preservation which presuppose an immediate threat from an agent who intends ... to kill or seriously injure you, and which themselves consist of immediate counter-attacks directed at that agent and at no-one else' (Teichman, 1986, p. 84). For example, in another hypothetical case, Meg attempts to kill Sam because she wants to take his money. So Meg points a gun she is carrying at Sam and pulls the trigger with the intention that shooting Sam will kill him. If Sam shoots Meg first in order to defend himself, then he is justified in acting in self-defence. But if Sam was to grab hold of an innocent bystander – Bobby – and use him as a human shield to protect himself from Meg's attack, then this would be an act of self-preservation but *not* justified self-defence. Sam unjustly sacrifices Bobby's life as a means to save himself. The upshot here is that self-preservation is not sufficient by itself to be considered morally justified self-defence.

There are a number of reasons why we should be careful to reject the view that one's life being at stake is sufficient justification for killing. First, in situations where lives are at stake, there should be limits on the actions one can take to preserve lives. Thomson (2008, p. 373) asks us to consider a case she calls 'Transplant' where a medical doctor has the opportunity to save the lives of five sick patients by killing and removing the organs of one healthy man. The preservation of the five lives in this case does not justify killing the healthy man. A second problem with the self-preservationist view is its failure to prohibit harm to innocent bystanders in situations of mortal danger. As described above, we might imagine a situation where Meg is shooting at Sam and the only way Sam can save his own life is by pushing Bobby, an innocent bystander who happens to be within reach, into the line of fire. This act of self-preservation is morally impermissible because it uses an innocent human life as a mere means to an end (Rachels, 1986, p. 128). A third problem with a self-preservationist account of killing in self-defence is the concern that it reduces morality in conflict to brute force. If we accept this approach to killing in self-defence, then moral justification becomes simply a matter of who is the strongest in the moment to survive. But not just anything goes in self-defence. As Thomson (1991, p. 305) points out, we cannot simply say that 'all bets are off when you will otherwise die'. She argues that the premise 'A will otherwise die' is not sufficient for the conclusion that A may kill B. One's life being threatened is a necessary but not solely sufficient condition to justify killing in self-defence: there needs to be something more to make an act of self-preservation count as morally justified killing in self-defence. That is, there must be a moral difference (i.e. moral asymmetry) between the two parties that counts (Ford, 2022).

In short, Fabre's partiality account blurs the bright line requiring a defender to establish that there is a relevant moral asymmetry between himself and a deadly threat. The defender should not have permission to kill others to save his own life simply because it is his life at stake. After all, both parties are likely to value their own lives. For example, imagine a situation where Meg unjustly attacks Sam. She attempts to shoot him but misses. This gives Sam enough time to shoot back at Meg in self-defence. Unfortunately for Sam, he also misses, which gives Meg the opportunity to take a second shot. She hits Sam and kills him. Meg can now argue that she acted in self-defence because, according to the partiality approach, she has a right to prefer her own life over Sam's. This is the case even though Meg was the one who unjustly attacked Sam in the first place. Fabre acknowledges that partiality might allow an attacker to claim that he is acting justifiably in such cases. Her solution is to add a proviso that the defender cannot have provoked the attack (Fabre, 2009, pp. 154–155). But this still doesn't explain why the defender's preference trumps other moral considerations. What makes self-preference the overwhelmingly decisive factor? What about other potentially morally worthy considerations, such as the utility of the lives at stake or the ages of the people involved?

More importantly, it's not clear how a defender transfers the right to protect himself – on the basis of a special stake in his own life – to a third party. The egoist condition, as expressed by Fabre (2009), says that one must be directly threatened by the target of one's self-defensive actions (p. 153). On the face of it, this rules out the partiality justification in defence of others. So, for example, a parent could kill an attacker in his own self-defence but not in defence of his child. A parent attempting to intervene using lethal force against an attacker to protect his child would then be morally liable to defensive force himself, which would be an absurd result. So a fundamental flaw in Fabre's account is lack of clarity about the mechanism for transferring the moral permissibility to kill in self-defence from the potential victim of an unjust attack to someone capable of intervening.

CONCLUSION

A third party should use forceful intervention (including lethal force) to protect an innocent human life in cases where the use of force against an unjust threat is morally permissible and the intervener has a duty to rescue the victim's life.

This humanitarian duty includes forcefully intervening when: (1) we are capable of intervening; (2) our intervention is necessary to prevent the wrongful death of an innocent human; and (3) intervention is *not* unreasonably risky or costly. Furthermore, the moral permissibility of forcefully intervening is built on a principle of impartialism. All other things being equal, a third party must satisfy the same impartial moral requirements that hold for self-defence. In the absence of an impartial moral justification, an intervener who uses lethal force is liable to defensive force himself. If this is correct, then it is *morally obligatory* for the intervener (Dean) to kill the attacker (Meg) in order to rescue the victim (Sam) when it is morally permissible to kill Meg and: (1) Dean is capable of intervening to rescue Sam's life; (2) Dean's intervention is necessary to prevent Sam's wrongful death; and (3) Dean's intervention is *not* unreasonably risky and/or costly to himself.

NOTES

1. Although I cannot address this debate here at any length, I will note that a view which holds that human life is no more valuable than other forms of life, strikes me as implausible if it puts a human life morally on par with that of bacteria.
2. A potential problem with basing the intrinsic value of human life on personhood, however, is that it might not include selves who lack a sufficient level of normative agency, such as infants and the severely mentally retarded. But when we talk about defending the lives of others, I am presuming that most people would include children as proper subjects of rescue. Infants have the capacity to become persons and, under normal conditions, will become persons (whereas bacteria and puppies do not have the underlying capacity and thus will not become persons). And severely mentally retarded people are human beings with damaged underlying capacity and, therefore, diminished properties of persons (as opposed to not having those properties at all).
3. This is not a comment on the intrinsic worth or otherwise of animals. Rather it is to suggest that animals require a distinct moral analysis. In other words, 'human rights' are the wrong category to imbue animals with intrinsic value.
4. There are also likely to be a raft of broader issues relating to the problem of 'vigilantism'. But I will not address those issues here.

REFERENCES

Bellamy, A. J. (2014). *The responsibility to protect: A defense*. Oxford University Press.
Bevir, M., & Hall, I. (2020). Interpreting the English school: History, science and philosophy. *Journal of International Political Theory*, *16*(2), 120–132.
Chesterman, S. (2011). "Leading from Behind": The responsibility to protect, the Obama Doctrine, and humanitarian intervention after Libya. *Ethics & International Affairs*, *25*(03), 279–285.
Dobos, N. (2011). *Insurrection and intervention: The two faces of sovereignty*. Cambridge University Press.
Doyle, M. W. (2011). International ethics and the responsibility to protect. *International Studies Review*, *13*(1), 72–84.
Dworkin, R. (1993). *Life's dominion: An argument about abortion and euthanasia*. Harper Collins.
Fabre, C. (2007). Mandatory rescue killings. *Journal of Political Philosophy*, *15*(4), 363–384.
Fabre, C. (2009). Permissible rescue killings. *Proceedings of the Aristotelian Society*, *109*(2), 149–164.
Finnemore, M. (1996). Constructing norms of humanitarian intervention. In P. J. Katzenstein (Ed.), *The culture of national security: Norms and identity in world politics* (319–325). Columbia University Press.
Fletcher, G. P. (1990). Defensive force as an act of rescue. *Social Philosophy and Policy*, *7*(02), 170–179.

Ford, S. B. (2022). Rights-based justifications for self-defense: Defending a modified unjust threat account. *International Journal of Applied Philosophy*, *36*(1), 49–65.
Gert, B. (1967). Hobbes and psychological egoism. *Journal of the History of Ideas*, *28*(4), 503–520.
Gorr, M. (1990). Private defense. *Law and Philosophy*, *9*(3), 241–268.
Griffin, J. (2008). *On human rights*. Oxford University Press, Inc.
Hobbes, T. (1996 [1651]). Leviathan. In R. Tuck (Ed.), *Hobbes: Leviathan* (pp. 1–618). Revised student edition. Cambridge University Press.
Ignatieff, M. (2021). The responsibility to protect in a changing world order: Twenty years since its inception. *Ethics and International Affairs*, *35*(2), 177–180.
James, S. M. (2007). Good samaritans, Good humanitarians. *Journal of Applied Philosophy*, *24*(3), 238–254.
Kuperman, A. J. (2013). A model humanitarian intervention? Reassessing NATO's Libya campaign. *International Security*, *38*(1), 105–136.
Locke, J. (1988 [1689]). *Two treatises of government*. Cambridge University Press.
McMahan, J. (2005). The basis of moral liability to defensive killing. *Philosophical Issues*, *15*(1), 386–405.
McMahan, J. (2009). *Killing in war*. Oxford University Press.
Nagel, T. (1991). *Equality and partiality*. Oxford University Press.
Pattison, J. (2010). *Humanitarian intervention and the responsibility to protect: Who should intervene?* Oxford University Press.
Rachels, J. (1986). *The elements of moral philosophy*. McGraw-Hill, Inc.
Singer, P. (1972). Famine, affluence, and morality. *Philosophy & Public Affairs*, *1*(3), 229–243.
Teichman, J. (1986). *Pacifism and the just war: A study in applied philosophy*. Basil Blackwell.
Thomson, J. J. (1991). Self-defense. *Philosophy & Public Affairs*, *20*(4), 283–310.
Thomson, J. J. (2008). Turning the trolley. *Philosophy & Public Affairs*, *36*(4), 359–374.
Weiss, T. G. (2012). *Humanitarian intervention*. Polity.
Wheeler, N. J. (2000). *Saving strangers: Humanitarian intervention in international society*. Oxford University Press.

CHAPTER 6

HOW AN ETHICS OF CARE CAN TRANSFORM CORPORATE LEADERSHIP: THE LAYERED ROUND TABLE APPROACH

Larelle Bossi[a] and Lonnie Bossi[b]

[a]*Institute for Ethics Governance and Law, Griffith University, Australia*
[b]*Executive Committee, Australian Association for Professional and Applied Ethics*

ABSTRACT

Since the COVID-19 pandemic, many have argued that we require transformational leadership to help us face the challenges of the Fourth Industrial Revolution (4thIR). The authors propose the layered round table approach to be one response to this call to arms. Inspired by the hierarchical, systematised, impersonal, and transactional interactions of the military, the boardroom table (or traditional corporate organisational structures) has largely continued to reflect Max Weber's bureaucratic theory of management 150 years ago. Whilst the round table has symbolised inclusivity and diversity, the authors argue that it has not quite displaced the exploitative tendencies of hierarchical management styles. Whilst most board rooms have introduced the round table to encourage discussions and debate, solutions are still largely decided upon by CEOcracies or expert advisors. In this chapter, the authors aim to lift the round table from out of the sphere of the symbolic, clarify these challenges, and posit ways in overcoming them via the layered round table approach. More than a symbol of inclusion and communion, it becomes the hub of solution creation and ensures the kind of transformational leadership required to face today and tomorrow. The authors present the layered round table as the seat from which managers can build the kind of cultural change which fosters more nurturing values, far removed from the mechanistic legacy of our corporate genealogy/past.

Keywords Ethics of care; ethical round table; courage and compassion; solution creation; transformational leadership

1. INTRODUCTION

First coined by James V. Downton in 1973, 'transformational leadership' is a concept less about transactional relationships and more about moral virtues and the impact visionaries have on their followers. It is unsurprising that Downton's transformational leader reflects his own religious commitments and is most effectively personified by religious influencers like Martin Luther King. In more recent years, the literature has focussed on transformative leadership as a leadership approach that focusses on inspiring positive change, fostering innovation, and promoting ethical behaviour within organisations. Whilst transformational leaders may inspire, empower, and stimulate followers to exceed standard expectations of performance, it does not follow that transformational impacts are ever fully realised or achieved. Everywhere we turn, there is crisis: climate, humanitarian, displacement, environmental, pandemic, biodiversity, inequity, mental health and health, economic, food security, gender violence ... existential! It seems inadequate to be dedicating our time to discussions on transformational leadership and decision making but it is precisely in this lacking for which we find ourselves here at all – paralysed by crisis. This chapter is dedicated to reimagining *transformative leadership* at the tables from which they are seated. We propose rethinking of the values and cultural legacy of the respective rectangular and round tables. We consider a way to overcome the challenges faced by both the linear and circular character of each through a kind of symbolic squaring of the circle motif, so that we may more harmoniously face the challenges today and the adversity of tomorrow.

2. THE BOARDROOM TABLE: NARCISSISTIC LEADERSHIP OR MILITARY RELIC

At the head of a long expensive table lined with attentive ears wearing suits, John Tuld, CEO and Chairman of the Board, inculcates everyone into his culture of Friedman*esque* economic liberalism (Friedman, 1962) – from the emerging managers to seasoned C-suite executives. In the 2011 release Margin *Call*, Jeremy Irons is at his best as an intimidating and razor-sharp business leader. He doesn't give you a warm fuzzy feeling, but he's straight to the point and clear about what he expects from the people around him. His motives may be less than noble, but he does embody the characteristics of a powerful leader in his boardroom. I stipulate *his* because he sits at the head of the long table and commands the attention of his working group invited to support him, in sycophantic harmony – his intentions and his motivations. Even if you do not recall the 'I tell you, this is it!' scene, or have not seen this particular film, you must be familiar with any one of the conservative boardroom scenes – men in dark suits (usually also with the token female) sitting in rank around a large, expensive rectangular table. Not just any table, its length, and design represent the success, wealth, and values of the company – often crafted from old growth wood of deep mahogany or ebony, or rare and protected Huon pine, or even the reclaimed and repurposed wood of a historical shipwreck!

PTC dedicates a page on their website (White, 2019) to show just how they connected their global headquarters building at Boston Seaport to the past with an 'incredible 22-foot boardroom table made from wood salvaged from a ... 19th century two-mastered schooner'. Dickey was the local *Timber Guy* (2011) tasked with reclaiming and transforming the remains of the ship estimated to be 100 around the time it was shipwrecked from out of the mud of the former South Boston Flats (Wu, 2017), and into a corporate treasure. The *Seaport Shipwreck* boardroom table in both material and design reflects the shipping legacy of the city of Boston and the location of PTCs new global headquarters. You could say that PTCs boardroom table has been crafted by the history of the very city of Boston itself and personifies its seafaring forefathers. Can the board room table – its size, shape, materiality, and use reflect the culture of an organisation – especially within a time that seems to be increasingly replacing this linear metaphor with the round table as a seat for transformational leadership and cultural change?

2.1. Chain of Command

When we think about Chairman Tuld at his boardroom table, we see a paternal image that is all too familiar with hierarchical structures. Like all other pyramidal chains of command, Tuld could be a General or CEO respectively at the top with his sergeants, corporal, and privates or senior executives, managers, and floor workers *en masse* positioned at the base. In simple terms, the chain of command is the succession of leader through which command is exercised and executed. We are surely all too familiar with Colonel Jessep's order of the code red (Reiner, 1992) in *A Few Good Men*! These structures are also not born from capitalism and precede even the First Industrial Revolution (1st IR) – feudal systems, governments, Norse mythology, Catholic Papal Palace, educational institutions, business management – and of course they have almost always been the structure of how we have gone to battle.

We are certainly not the first to compare the paternalistic, hierarchical structure of the corporate organisation to that of the military. In his landmark *The Practice of Management*, the Austrian-American business author and consultant, Peter Drucker (1954) wrote 'The first systematic book on leadership: the Kyropaidaia of Xenophon – himself no mean leader of men – is still the best book on the subject'. Xenophon wrote the biography, around 200 years after Cyrus the Great used military conquest and enlightened governance to create the first Persian Empire around 540 BC. It inspired his own leading of the march of the 10,000 for which he became most known. Dissatisfied by the tales of this epic event, Xenophon published his own account of the event with himself as the central figure. In the third book of this journey, the 10,000 soldiers found themselves in dire straits, largely precipitated by previous leaders who exhibited various levels of treachery and extreme autocratic behaviour. Xenophon explains how the men were far away from home, surrounded by enemies, almost without supplies, and very demoralised. The soldiers at this point were a 'disorganized mass of individually helpless atoms' (Howland, 2000, p. 881). Under Xenophon's leadership, however, and with all the charisma of Downton's transformational leader, the community of the 10,000 was spared the horrors of complete disintegration and their salvation realised. In his characterisation of this philosophical odyssey, Howland (2000) contextualises Plato's Republic with Xenophon's military adventure to self-discovery. He demonstrates how the leader inspired his followers, by employing powerful terms and symbols, to become a motivated, unified force with high morale, a common goal, and a sense of purpose that transcended their individual self-interests (Howland, 2000). Xenophon stood apart from his predecessors in that he was able to look beyond the customs and conventions of the day that had limited their vision.

The story of Xenophon became part of the leadership syllabus for centuries for Alexander the Great and Julius Caesar. It continued to be a source of inspiration down the ages – influencing Machiavelli's *The Prince* and with Thomas Jefferson holding two copies in his library. Drucker resurrected a reimagining of Xenophon from military hero to Boardroom Chair and the very exemplar of leadership behaviour – charismatic and transformational. Humphreys and Einstein (2003) certainly place Xenophon as the cornerstone in the evolution of transformational leadership in both his display and narration (Grethlein, 2012) of behavioural range. They are keen to immortalise Xenophon as the transactional–transformational leader continuum. Bass and Avolio (1994) refer to the full range of leader behaviour (Humphreys & Einstein, 2003).

2.2. Transformations with Hierarchal Paternalism

When we think about hierarchical organisational structures, a simple formula can apply – one person generates strategy and gives orders. It is certainly interesting to reflect on the etymology of the word strategy when business management and leadership are so heavily dependent upon it. The term strategy (1810) comes from the French *stratégie* and directly from Greek *strategia* 'office or command of a general' from *strategos* 'general, commander of an army'. So much of the functioning of business corporate cultures involves strategies, underpinned by an almost infinite number of social, political, economic, environmental, and technological considerations, that challenge the efficacy of hierarchical paternalism.

Traditionally, a leader's unique perspective simply means that executives think, whilst everyone else follows orders. Leaders believed that bureaucracy (Weber, 1922) was the most efficient way to set up and manage a business organisation, and critical to enabling companies to achieve maximum productivity. Victory over the competition required a well-defined hierarchical management structure that delineated lines of communication and assigned responsibilities and authority. An employee who skipped levels to share an idea or concept risked a figurative court martial. It was career suicide to talk to your boss's boss or to do anything that might make your direct supervisor look bad. Today, both our corporate and public sector experiences are still largely characterised by the hierarchical, systematised, impersonal, and transactional interactions which have largely continued to reflect Max Weber's bureaucratic theory of management from 1922 – an almost 'blind adherence' to policies and procedures, standardised process, number of desks, and meticulous divisions of labour.

This chain of command has been proven time and again to be a successful way to lead a nation to victory in battle, or a company to execute strategies. Since Milton Friedman (1962) famously declared 'the social responsibility of business is to increase its profits' these hierarchical and paternalistic structures have efficiently promoted and successfully made free-market, shareholder primacy, and neoliberal philosophy the dominant global economic model. This has further promoted decision making firmly defined by short-sightedness, self-interest, and greed (limited to the tenure of those authorised with that decision-making power).

These exploitative measures are also mirrored in the interiority of an organisation, not only offshore but in our own Australian companies, institutions, and coalitions. Some of the leading global organisations continue to face interrogation for exploitative working conditions, modern slavery, and racial and sexual discrimination. We are faced with countless national royal commissions into corruption, mistreatment, and overworking of employees which make up the fabric of our society – our health and safety! We have witnessed the obliteration of First Nations culturally significant places by Australia's mining and energy interests. We have misogyny within our own federal government, and an inquiry into the sexual abuse of children in Tasmanian hospitals ... the list goes on and on and on!

The leaders of some of the world's biggest companies are more interested in zooming off the planet to another rock rotating around our sun or creating a deeper escape into a metaverse. If they are not trying to colonise space, or green and blue wash industries, they are striving to maintain their systems, structures, and power as they conveniently transition towards the next energy source to power our planet. Ought we really be expecting humane transformational change from the charismatic Musk, Bezos, Murdoch, our governments, vice chancellors, and managers during this 4thIR whose challenges are only eclipsed by the extraordinarily overwhelming human existential crisis? Amidst the number of crises we face, coupled with their complexity and multidisciplinary dimensions, hierarchical paternalism is unable to cultivate the kind of culture required for the kind of transformation humanity is demanding. We are certainly sceptical of the kinds of solutions created from a legacy so vulnerable to egoism and short-sightedness.

2.3. The Grandiose Narcissistic Leader

Whilst many management theorists have continued to reflect on Xenophon as a virtuous leader employing the full spectrum of leadership behaviours from the necessary to the noble, his biographical retelling of the march of the 10,000 seems to reflect a more recent recharacterisation of the charismatic leader as a pseudo-transformational narcissist (O'Reilly & Chatman, 2020; Sankowsky, 1995). They argue that transformational leaders challenge the status quo, provide a vision of a promising future, and motivate and inspire their followers to join in the pursuit of a better world (O'Reilly & Chatman, 2020). However, O'Reilly and Chatman (2020) say

> many of these leaders also fit the American Psychiatric Association classification for narcissistic personality disorder. They are grandiose, entitled, self-confident, risk seeking, manipulative, and hostile.

This certainly reflects some of the populist leaders of the more recent political climate and certainly supports the findings of the 27 psychiatrists and mental health experts assessing their president in *The Dangerous Case of Donald Trump* (2019) inspiring the Yale conference on the topic to ask, 'Does Professional Responsibility Include a Duty to Warn?' There have since been several reviews, articles, and books dedicated to the literature on narcissism and leadership in business which demonstrates how transformational leadership overlaps substantially with grandiose narcissism. O'Reilly and Chatman (2020) identify other narcissistic transformational leaders too – Steve Jobs, Travis Kalanik, Elizabeth Holmes, and Adam Neuman as well as those with malign intent like Hitler, Stalin, and Osama bin Laden. Characteristics of the narcissistic transformational leader include grandiosity, excessive self-confidence and risk seeking, entitled, manipulative and low integrity, hostility, and aggression. Each of the above-mentioned transformational leaders has a list of narcissistic examples from repeatedly parking in handicapped zones (Jobs), to investigations of criminal behaviour (Kalanik). Two studies illustrate how narcissistic CEOs' risk-seeking behaviour can lead to increased returns when the market is going up, but suffer larger losses when the market turns down (Buyl et al., 2019). The global financial crisis commencing in 2008 was commonly blamed on the 'greedy' and 'reckless' behaviour of bank CEOs, combined with poor corporate governance practices (DeYoung et al., 2013; Scott, 2011). They overinvest in good times and underinvest in the bad (Malmendier & Tate, 2005). Just as a gambler can go on a winning streak, narcissistic CEOs can appear brilliant for a while – but suffer in the end. There is certainly also a dictatorial quality to the narcissistic leader who would certainly perceive the decentralisation of decision making a sign of weakness and would see little need for building relationships or establishing connections. Nor do dictatorships require any real need for transparency. With this framework, the long, rectangular, and hard-edged boardroom table does not invite true debate and consideration from deeper within the organisation and the respective interactions with stakeholders.

Yet, there is no coincidence that Weber and Drucker and many others have found inspiration for transformational leadership in the ancient military leader, Xenophon. The willingness to challenge the status quo defines a transformational leader, and a narcissist's decisive leadership with a new vision can certainly provide a sense of psychological safety. It is also not surprising that charisma in a time of crisis begets followers, nor that grandiose narcissism climbs the corporate ladder right to the very top, carelessly discarding the hurdles that face them. The narcissist's self-confidence and willingness to go against the grain can be particularly attractive in uncertain times – entrepreneurial ventures, periods of disruption, crisis, or economic upheaval. Like Chairman Tuld, each requires the most heroic display of traditionally masculine values to attract followers from the head of his boardroom table. It is in some ways inevitable that narcissists are most likely to emerge as leaders, and that followers seek refuge within their promise of a future rooted in a dialogue of fearful consequences without their decisiveness and leadership. In our own time of crises within this 4thIR, desperately seeking transformational leadership, how do organisations really mitigate the inevitable and lasting negative impacts of narcissistic leaders within a rapidly changing environment? We agree with a key point made by O'Reilly and Chatman, and that is to cultivate an organisation with a culture that values teamwork, respect, and integrity more than individual achievement and success at any cost, but what good is our grave pursuit towards a change in culture or a legitimate transformational leader, when the main premise of the corporate activity and its traditionally paternalistic and hierarchical structure remains unchanged? Can we dare to introduce humanity within this rigid colossus that enables it to adapt and transform to the demands of its congregation?

2.4. The End of the Boardroom Table

In 1999, Benjamin Hermalin from Johnson Graduate School of Management drafted what most non-economists might question: whether 'economists know anything about culture' (Hermalin, 1999, 2012). It is certainly difficult to expect a flourishing, balanced, and inclusive culture from the kind of CEOcracies promoted by the grandiose narcissist leading the boardroom table, nor from the business classrooms of spreadsheets and analytics. There are many reasons for this lack of confidence: culture is not relevant in most economic modelling; culture is not quantifiable (or at least not obviously so) and, hence, does not fit well with the reductive methodology of neoclassical economics; and since culture is difficult to define or measure, it is difficult to use or control for in econometric analyses. Yet, like the current call to arms by so many authors since Hermalin (2012), we think transformational cultural change away from the expected is not only possible, but necessary.

Almost all accounting firms right now are advertising for cultural consultants, each trying to solve the 'culture problem' in organisations which (and to quote) sustain, promote, and celebrate 'big swinging dicks' (Liveris, 2022; Maiden, 2021; Pini, 2021). Yet, they generally fail to immerse themselves into the organisations, nor challenge the very framework and process of leadership that delivered their engagement for service, for fear of losing a very 'profitable workstream'. Similarly, whilst our references to paternalism and war are not a problem limited to just traditionally all-male, or dirty, or hard, or BIG-bucks industries, our characterisation of the boardroom table remains a reflection of the structures and power play within the hierarchical and paternalistic system that we have maintained since ancient military leadership. Persisting through from the businesses of the First Industrial Revolution, we continue to borrow, rather explicitly, from our long standing and historically significant military traditions of leadership. No matter how much we call for cultural consultants, or placard inclusive language around our open-plan offices, or try our darndest to weed out grandiose narcissism from legitimate transformational leaders, the long, rectangular, and hard-edged, boardroom table remains symbolic of the power held by the (all too often) man at the top of the hierarchy.

The most recent pressure from the COVID-19 pandemic however has certainly been felt by the greatest of CEOcracies. It appears that with greater force than any other social change movement – union, feminist, pride, #metoo, and black lives matter – the pandemic has generated a greater influence upon the narcissistic leaders, even if only instrumentally. It has been more recently demonstrated that firms led by narcissistic CEOs engage more actively in corporate social responsibility (CSR) or environmental social governance (ESG) efforts as a way to enhance their reputation and to save their corporate image (Al-Shammari et al., 2019)! Firms led by narcissistic CEOs purport to engage more actively in (CSR) efforts, albeit, when the hood is opened, often merely as tokenistic gestures, to repair reputations in brief spurts of bravado that more realistically reflect altruistic deception. True cultural transformation can only occur through a 'no strings attached' form of CSR or ESG, where activities are concurrently monitored independently of the organisational leadership.

3. THE ROUND TABLE: TRANSFORMATIONAL LEADERSHIP WITH CARE AND COURAGE

In his Roman de Brut, the Norman chronicler Wace, in 1155 was the first to mention the round table at which Arthur's knights met to prevent quarrels between his barons over the question of precedence. Others say it was more an amphitheatre built by the Romans to house 1,000 knights. Whether or not the round table was real, it has come to symbolise the change of paradigms during the Middle Ages. They were a difficult period to live in, there were barbarian hordes, wars, plague, famine, and many other threats. The normal way to get something was to take it by force. There was little to no value for the lives of individuals without power. Then, the development of chivalry played a role in shifting the belief systems of people. The round table shifted the power from just the king who gave all the orders. In that table, everyone had an equal say. Sure, the king was still the king, and the knights were still knights, but the shift was to the belief in the worth of the individual and diversity of opinion regardless of whether he held land or weapons.

Historically, the objectives of the Arthurian round table were to remove hierarchy, regardless of the forum of participants. The absence of the formal leadership position at the head of the table was a symbolic step towards pushing aside narcissistic and dictatorial tendencies, commonplace in monarchies and social institutions (equally applicable to the corporations of today). These meetings were not limited to knights alone, but inclusive of political, religious, and business leaders of the day, to encourage open and considered dialogue to resolve fundamental challenges and issues facing all interest groups. This seems to ring to the tune of the kind of big shift to a humane model of management leadership Gallo and Hlupik (2019) are calling to arms to face the 4thIR, and certainly documented within diagnostic medicine.

3.1. Diagnostic Efficiency and Success of the Round Table and Its Very Real Challenges

The use of the round table in evidence-based medical diagnostics has delivered efficient and effective outcomes (Alston & Whittenbury, 2013; Erba et al., 2017). Such published success stories can be found in sports medicine, health care quality, and genomics over the past 20 years with a significant increase in publications concerning outcomes in diagnostics from round tables in cardiovascular medicine since the COVID-19 pandemic (Alston & Whittenbury, 2013; Doehner et al., 2020; Elliott et al., 2020; Erba et al., 2017; Leclercq et al., 2022). The symbolic round table – often a virtual one – has transformed this space through the establishment of the Institute of Medicine (IOM) Roundtable on Evidence-based Medicine (2007), with the aim of supporting clinical decisions by accurate, timely, and up-to-date clinical information to reflect the best available evidence. The IOM Roundtable continues to serve as a forum to facilitate the collaborative assessment and action around issues central to achieving effective clinical outcomes for over 90% of clinical decisions. The pursuit of such collaborative outcomes and actions beyond the success of the medical round tables is however not without its challenges.

Whilst the round table is symbolic of the decision making and action processes of First Nations communities all over the world (The International Council on Monuments and Sites, 2023), its effectiveness and efficiency in corporate settings have been less than ideal with its greatest success in information generation and sharing. For example, a symbolic round table similar to the medical ones in Europe and across the USA was created 50 years ago also in the USA but within the corporate space. The *Business Roundtable* (BR) is an association of CEOs of the USA's leading companies in Washington DC. BR members work closely with policymakers from both political parties to advance sound economic policies to spur job creation, expand opportunity, and strengthen the USA's competitiveness. More a symbol of information generation than a transformative alternative to the boardroom table, this 50-year-old association is reflective of the kinds of challenges the round table as a symbol of transformational leadership and cultural change really poses to the corporate organisation. External to the success of medical diagnostics and like the BR, the round table is often applied at conventions and industry forums and is typically a collection of interested leaders discussing a key issue that is impacting each interest group differently. The participants are often subject matter experts (SME) or senior representatives, that present from a personal or organisational perspective with limited commitment to action or follow-up in a collaborative or consolidated manner, but rather, to gather intel to further their own self-interest – knowledge, research, copyright, etc. In short, the corporate round tables discuss sectarian*esque* views within a broader scope, resolve little, and commit even less to resources.

The round table discussions, debates, and think-tanks of today are not the most desired outcomes in companies, perceived as taking up time and money and not delivering results to shareholders and board members – even if they are committed to shaking off Milton Friedman's pursuit to profits as the business social driver! Other times, round tables reach stale mates or resolution impotence. A round table supports inclusion, diversity, and ideas of equality and too often ethical decision making is stifled by ideas of cultural sensitivities or out of fear of offending the other. Outside of ethics departments, cultural relativism is too often confused for the ethical and so the less narcissistic stop short of any kind of judgement at all. This certainly was the case at a recent round table we attended concerning human impacts on our oceans. Even if they are inspired by action, the momentum to resolve around this kind of round table is lacking any *chutzpah* or courage at all – drawing only knowledge production to a close in the end. Perhaps the character of the round table is too esoteric an ideal in! More to the point, we may be too quick to remove leadership from the table all together. Arthur of course stood amongst others at the round table, which prompts us to question the kind of leader required at this circular table. Whilst it is not the narcissist, we can agree that it is also not one lacking in charisma all together. Gallo, Hlupic, and Asbari called for humane leadership – a humanist with a moral radar – to face the 4thIR (Asbari, 2020; Gallo & Hlupic, 2019). Is the leader of the round table also a humanist?

3.2. Humanist Leadership: Is Aristotle Enough?

Humanism is a system of education and mode of inquiry that originated during the 13th and 14th centuries in northern Italy. By the 15th century, *i umanisti* were professors and students of classical studies in grammar, poetry, rhetoric, history, and moral philosophy. A derivative of Cicero's concept of *humanitas*, humanists believe that humans are capable of discovering truths about the world and humanity's place within it. The universe is a natural phenomenon discerned by the senses of the humanist and behaving according to principles that can be observed, determined, predicted, and described. Humanists are meaning makers which is to say they make their own purpose in life, set their own goals, and give meaning to their own life. Free from a supernatural metaphysics, humanism is certainly reflected in Aristotle's commitment to rationalism and his system of ethics based on human nature (Law, 2011).

The development of human virtues was defined by the character of the universe humanists observed. Whilst Aristotle was by no means the only ancient Greek humanist, the revival of his work on the golden mean has certainly attracted attention in business ethics and transformative leadership discourse in more recent times. The ancient Greek pursuit of 'the good life' was documented in ethical dialogues which define human happiness to chiefly consist in practising the virtues, a life in which both desire and the pursuit of wealth is kept under check.

For Aristotle, *eudaimonia* (personal happiness) was achieved by making appropriate use of our capacities and leading a life in which we are optimally functioning in accord with our purpose as human beings (Bragues, 2006). Purpose was not granted by a divinity but consistent with humanists, purpose was self-made. According to Aristotle, virtue reaches its height with the exercise of the intellectual virtues of prudence and wisdom – manifesting in leadership and the philosophical search for truth, respectively. In his 'Seek the Good Life and Not Money', George Bragues (2006) details just how 'from an Aristotelian point of view, the greatest ethical imperative for business is to give individuals opportunities to thoughtfully participate in the management of company affairs and to contemplate the ultimate meaning of things' (p. 341). More recently, Levine and Boaks (2014) demonstrate how leadership can and should be grounded in a *eudaimonic* framework using the conceptual framework that Aristotle provides (p. 241). This is not prescriptive but rather insistent on a kind of relativism, understood as situation dependent or situational. With an appeal to soft universalism, we also consider the characteristics of the *eudaimonic* leader at the round table to motivate the kind of resolutions we need.

A *eudaimonic* round table founded by the golden mean entails a leadership of moderation beholden to the virtues flanked by vices of excess and deficiencies. Before we consider this imperative to the modern leader, we need to make clear the operational expectations of a corporate leader. All things being equal, a leader requires the following skills: **vision** to provide a direction and platform to achieve success; **strategic aptitude** to lead the process of developing and executing the plan for success; **communication capability** to simplify and clarify messaging to match the demands of the recipients of the message; and **coaching**, which incorporates, talent identification, managing people, and role modelling. Such skills could quite easily be translated into the military, academic, or political arenas.

To support these varied skills, there are numerous virtues we have identified that a leader requires to develop a coherent and committed community at the round table which meets the aims of our transformational leaders today and tomorrow: **interconnection, information transparency, technical assistance**, and **decentralised decisions**. Some of the virtues we have identified are explicitly Aristotelian and others are in the spirit of eudaimonia in so far as they require a moderate character.

Flanked by cowardice and rashness, **courage** is a powerful virtue, for a leader to be innovative and make the just and tough decisions when required. Inevitably, this will challenge stakeholders, but importantly, be the cornerstone of many of the virtues which follow. We will revisit courage as a cornerstone in the kind of leader we require at the round table in Section 3.3. **Truthfulness** is certainly one of Aristotle's virtues which we think is related to the contemporary need for transparency. Whilst truthfulness is a personal virtue beholden by the leader and the participants of the round table, transparency begins to move into the realm of the group and the corporate community at large. **Transparency**, therefore, can be the most challenging to consistently uphold, when the objectives of the round table continue to broaden.

Transparency requires a strong dose of **humility** – rather distinct from Aristotle's modesty. Whilst modesty tends to focus on the perception a leader may present, humility focusses on the interior character of a leader. Whilst modesty is flanked by shyness and shamelessness, we argue that humility is flanked by narcissism and diffidence. A humble leader encourages interconnectivity of all stakeholders, particularly where the power imbalance leans in favour of the leader. It fosters the building of strong and lasting relationships and ensures that the leader remains humane and connectable to people.

Oftentimes, leaders, particularly narcissistic ones, will dominate conversation, however, it is only through a respect for **reciprocity**, that a leader better understands the sometimes-concealed factors that impact decisions and facilitates more balanced dialogue and interactions to occur. This certainly requires the leader to develop listening skills when speaking is too often the expectation. This is also reflected in the famous aphorism by the stoic thinker Epictetus, who has been argued to have also been influenced by Aristotle's *Nicomachean Ethics*. We have two ears and one mouth so that we can listen twice as much as we speak.

Commonly clustered values of **respect**, **trust**, and **integrity** are fundamental to humanist leadership and are the bedrock of the kind of judgement and alignment demanded of a humanist leader. To build trust and respect in an organisation or community, one must also embrace humility, transparency, and courage to ensure relationships are formed on solid footing. Meanwhile, integrity comes back to the leader's ethical stance, their courage in the face of challenge, and their commitment to relationships that they impact.

Many will consider loyalty as a cornerstone of leadership; however, we argue that there is little place for loyalty for a leader. Blind loyalty often results in sycophantic behaviours and the development of cohorts or cronyism, which result in restricted dialogue, poor decision making, and often an absence of courage. **Commitment**, on the other hand, supports psychological safety, the environment to challenge a leader's authority and perspectives, and yet, with a transparent communication framework, will enable teams to thrive and both current and future leaders to develop. A leader must commit to the journey, rather than the agreed plan, as their team must also commit to play their role, which includes to challenge, rather than loyally follow. As certain as change is, so too are factors that require pathways to be modified, people to disagree and both the group and the individual to evolve. Of course, the leader first must be humble and courageous enough to welcome such commitment.

Resilience is another virtue we believe to be a pillar of the humanist, with the flanked vices of rigidity and frailty. Crisis requires an agile mind to overcome natural disasters, war, famine, pandemics, inequalities, and the contemplations of a new kind of leadership, a new kind of corporate approach. The battles a leader will face, on behalf of their team, will be in what are often termed 'pits of vipers' where the leader must relinquish the benefit of the self, for the good of the community they represent. Resilience and courage stand arm in arm when the rampart is challenged – whether it is the humanist leader or the community they serve.

Finally, the leader must **inspire** their people, and with that comes a healthy dose of **charisma**, competency, courage, humility, **compassion**, and respect. To empower and engage a community of followers, the leader must be willing to risk failure, then accept that errors will occur, and must ultimately be willing to hand the baton to capable emerging leaders that they helped cultivate. Leaders of the round table must have compassion for the people, the situations, and the community that they impact, to understand their place and circumstance. To inspire, the leader must put the welfare of the group ahead of the self and embody an ethics of care. How can we even contemplate an ethics of care within an organisation, which to this point, we have characterised as being controlled by narcissistic, self-interested, egoistical, and profit-driven mad men?

It is this focus on the group over the self which exposes the limitations of Aristotelian leadership at the round table. In the end, Aristotle calls for the exploitation of man's highest faculty – the mind – to sustain personal happiness. And yes, we specify man, because his virtue ethics were the attributes espoused by Greek men. Interestingly, the word virtue comes from the Latin 'vir' for man. It also stems from the Greek concept of *aretē* from the Greek god Ares – warrior like. As a product of his time and place, Aristotle's virtues certainly reflected the masculine ideals of the day, particularly those of what were the living aims of male Greek citizens. Moral decision making is expected to be rational, with a focus on universal and objective considerations. There is no room for traditionally feminine values empathy, caring, community, or emotional intelligence. Aristotle's virtues not only assume a staunch dichotomy between reason and the emotions but also between the personal and the collective. At a table that encourages a focus on community, Aristotle's pursuit to personal happiness, even if virtuous, falls short of meeting the moral expectations of the round table.

According to Brian Ellis (2011), morality should aim for *eudaimonia*, an Aristotelian concept that combines a satisfying life with virtue and happiness by improving societies worldwide. It is important to note that Ellis has applied Aristotelian thinking to the broader community, and so has a rather generous interpretation of *eudaimonic* principles. The welfare of the other as a collective, or a group, or a community requires us to think about leadership in a slightly different way. It encourages more feminine values like emotional intelligence, empathy, compassion, and care to be brought to the round table.

Since Martha Nussbaum (1992) first argued that emotions have their valuable place in ethics we have become more accepting to the way in which some emotions can be reasonable, morally appropriate, and even helpful in guiding good decisions or actions (Caggiano & Ragusa, 2022). Feminist ethics also recognises that rules must be applied in a context, and real-life moral decision making is influenced by the relationships we have with those around us. *I umaniti* were not only committed to social criticism but also the painstaking reassessments of history and the bold reshaping of the future. In short, humanism called for the comprehensive reform of culture, and even transformational leadership. Surely, humanism today would call for a reform of the paternalistic hierarchy with a masculine preference. If we are to build a round table, inclusive, diverse, and equal, the humane leader we require surely needs to meet an ethics of care.

After all, this is not a man versus woman question, or one about which gender sits in leadership at the Arthurian round table, but a question of a common humanity.

3.3. Ethics of Care Creates a Culture of Care from the Round Table

It is one thing to call to arms a transformative leader with an ethical and humane character, but it is altogether another to do so in a hierarchical structure. Before we consider this kind of assault on the status quo, it is useful to consider that the round table by geometry is a circle. Pitched against the patriarchal boardroom table, the round variety is not short of feminine character. It is curvy and unyielding. It is also unsurprising that the round table's rise to prominence has been under virtual conditions. Its very shape is symbolic of the striving to connect and come together when we are otherwise isolated, individuated, and alone. In hope of connecting through the *aether*, the virtual round table is elusive in essence, yet inclusive whether your camera is switched on or off. The circle is a universal symbol which can mean timelessness, the eternal, the infinite, original perfection, and other transcendental and sublime concepts. This is not to assume that the Arthurian table has been hijacked by women, as much as a female CEO will not sit at the head of the traditional boardroom table. Rather, this is where the circle defines a potential that is beyond traditional gender-values. In the end, these tables are a reflection of the character of a culture which happens to reflect traditionally masculine or feminine values (Table 6.1). But even in a symbolic sense, the circle, whilst less forgiving is not exclusively feminine.

Hermes Trismegistus said 'God is a circle whose center is everywhere and whose circumference is nowhere'. This seems to confirm our ambitions of the round table in business as seeking the impossible, but perhaps the circle, in all its ephemerality can come to symbolise the union of opposites. Just as the circle of life symbolises life and death, perhaps the corporate round table can similarly come to symbolise the power and strength in diversity, as much as it can represent the safety and stability in change and flux.

If the corporate round table is going to be transformative in action creation, then it needs to embody the character of the circle. It is not sitting in the pursuit of individual needs, but rather as a collective. In a more practical sense, consider a round table, where the leadership responsibilities fall not to the most senior or influential members of the round table, but one espousing the virtues of leadership, that has been identified as a future leader, and has garnered the respect of those around them. All members of the round table must sit in **humility**, for not only the leader in this round table, but more critically, for any who believe they are superior to the leader, whether it be in seniority, subject matter expertise, remuneration, and/or connectivity within the organisation or beyond. With leadership must come a sense of comfort in accepting that your role and influence is temporary, and that you are merely a custodian of the business and its decision making. The broader this sphere of realisation grows, the more ethical, inclusive, considered, and insightful becomes the decision-making process and its outcomes, and the more humanist the leadership style is cultivated. It is certainly expected that with humility, the most inspirational leader at any given round table may also exercise enough trust, commitment, and courage to remove themselves entirely from the process and provide a more guiding, nurturing, and developmental mentorship in the process. In borrowing a military term, many leaders will see themselves as mercenaries – well paid, self-interested survivors, and asked to undertake ethically challenged situations. But are they a general or a soldier? Should their existence be one of the self or of the many? We, therefore, propose that for the kind of transformational leadership we require to face the challenges of our world in crisis, and to banish the rise of narcissists, the corporate round table needs to be nestled within and nurtured by an ethics of care.

Feminist ethics and the ethics of care have significantly contributed to discussions on ethical leadership in business by emphasising relationality, empathy, and inclusivity in decision-making processes. These ethical frameworks offer alternative perspectives that challenge traditional, male-centric models of leadership and promote a more holistic approach to ethical decision making within organisations. Feminist ethics extends beyond gender differences to provide pathways for recognising, evaluating, and addressing ethical issues in business contexts (Borgerson, 2007). By emphasising care, cooperation, and relationality, feminist ethics offers a unique lens through which ethical leadership can be understood and practised. This approach aligns with the principles of ethical leadership, which involve demonstrating broad ethical awareness and concern for outcomes beyond mere financial interests (Akrivou et al., 2011). Similarly, the ethics of care, as discussed by Cingöz and Akdoğan (2019), focusses on compassion, context, and relationships rather than impartiality and universal standards. This perspective underscores the importance of considering the well-being of all stakeholders and fostering a culture of care and empathy within organisations. It is argued by feminist ethicists in business that by integrating the ethics of care into discussions on ethical leadership, business leaders can cultivate environments that prioritise ethical behaviour, social responsibility, and stakeholder well-being. Overall, feminist ethics and the ethics of care offer valuable insights into ethical leadership practices by emphasising the significance of relationships, compassion, and ethical decision making that goes beyond traditional profit-driven approaches. By incorporating these ethical frameworks into leadership practices, organisations can promote a more inclusive, empathetic, and socially responsible approach to business ethics.

3.4. The Problem of a Round Table in a Rectangular System

The corporate round table, its culture, and leadership teams are required to first remember their humanity and then also be ethically driven. We propose an upgrade of what we have traditionally considered feminine values in the workplace. A focus on building relationships, creating safe spaces for discussions, and encouraging self-development and work–life balance are not a tick the box exercise but the foundations of a flourishing community and corporate culture. Leaders who embrace the ethics of care demonstrate genuine concern for their employees and broader stakeholder community. They go beyond traditional profit-driven approaches and focus on creating a culture of compassion, support, and ethical decision making within the organisation (Brown & Treviño, 2006;

Kalshoven et al., 2011; Walumbwa et al., 2007). Ethical leaders who embody the ethics of care are characterised by their ability to demonstrate normatively appropriate conduct through personal actions and interpersonal relationships. They promote ethical behaviour by engaging in two-way communication, reinforcing ethical standards, and involving employees in decision-making processes (Walumbwa et al., 2007). These leaders are honest, trustworthy, caring, and fair in their interactions, which fosters positive attitudes amongst followers and contributes to a culture of respect and integrity within the organisation (Brown & Treviño, 2006).

However, challenges arise when the patriarchy still holds sway in business environments. In patriarchal structures, traditional gender norms and power dynamics may undermine the implementation of the ethics of care. Gender biases and stereotypes can hinder the recognition of caring behaviours as valuable leadership qualities, leading to a lack of support for leaders who prioritise empathy and relationality (Jia et al., 2020). Patriarchal systems may perpetuate a focus on individualism, competition, and profit maximisation, which can conflict with the values of care, cooperation, and inclusivity promoted by the ethics of care (Kristinsson et al., 2024), or further, conflict with the objective of longer-term corporate and cultural sustainability. In such environments, leaders who advocate for the ethics of care may face resistance or scepticism from those accustomed to hierarchical and authoritative leadership styles.

The American psychologist Carol Gilligan (1982) influenced the 1980s evaluation of working within a 'man's world' (p. 548). The paternalistic hierarchical structure of the military inspired corporate culture is certainly still a man's world (in value and mindset, not necessarily in gender). Whilst the pandemic has done wonders in shifting this picture, we can agree that the rise of narcissistic leaders in a world where women are still battling glass ceilings, equal pay, competitive and isolating factions, and the overworked fatigue of family demands, the notion of a feminist corporate culture is whilst what we may need, almost certainly out of reach! At the same time, many women at the top of the corporate hierarchy have not themselves cultivated an ethics of care in their leadership styles but have done their best at perpetuating the male-centric values of self-interest, competitiveness, and profit-maximisation. Whilst Gilligan's work was influential in accepting the cultural differences between boys and girls, we think there has also been enough research and development since her *In a Different Voice* (1980) within the feminist literature to also show that an ethics of care is beneficial for all genders. In the end, we have all suffered from the paternalistic hierarchical structures around us and are all in need of a good dose of care and opportunity for healing.

In society, an ethics of care is often referred to as a culture of care, a lived experience increasingly exposed by the media in its stories of failed culture: banking non-compliance; mining company's environmental and cultural destructiveness; casinos governance failures; sexual harassment in political corridors; the exploitation of the casual army in universities; the 'nocturnal activities' of the clergy; or media's harassment culture itself. Yet, not until recently, did the arrow of blame get pointed to the lack of care, best highlighted in growing discourse relating to mental health and occupational health and safety practices littered throughout industries globally. It is not just that society is increasingly demanding care to be at the centre of decisions but that if workforce and trade are going to sustain, all the models necessarily require us to increasingly place care in the central node of our processes, values, and decision making. The voices of social movements over the past centuries have finally infiltrated their way into the corporate system, once immune from the pressures of politics and social justice, now being held accountable by them – a correlational response to the CSR necessitated by neoliberalism (Bossi, 2023).

3.5. Towards an Eudaimonic Round Table Community

Overcoming the challenges of the patriarchal legacy requires a shift in organisational culture towards valuing empathy, collaboration, and social responsibility. Leaders must actively work to dismantle patriarchal structures, promote gender equality, and create inclusive spaces where the ethics of care can thrive (Kang, 2019; Lee & Hoe, 2022). By addressing these challenges and promoting the ethics of care in leadership practices, organisations can cultivate environments that prioritise ethical behaviour, employee well-being, and sustainable business practices. Leaders who embrace the ethics of care contribute to creating a more compassionate, equitable, and socially responsible business landscape.

At the round table, guided by *eudaimonic* virtues and caring leadership, we ultimately replace shareholder primacy with stakeholder balance, where all stakeholders get a chance to not only impact decision making but, in fact, lead in its contribution. Instead of asking the moral decision-maker to be unbiased, the caring moral agent will consider that one's duty may be greater to those with whom they share particular bonds, or to others who are powerless rather than powerful. Care ethics advises us to meet others where they are, in their particularity.

An ethics of care makes the nurturing of our immediate communities and the protecting of those closest to us the highest moral obligation. In business, an ethics of care asks us to review decisions not in terms of hard rules but in terms of how they will affect the people with whom we share our lives. The most important stakeholder of any organisation is thus always its people, **the employees**. They are responsible for the work, connect with customers, facilitate organisational goals, in some instances are also the customers, or if not, the neighbours of customers, the strongest advocates, and yet can undermine 'the brand' by a single word. They are the voters of governments and are socially engaged. The humanist leader not only knows this but is best prepared to engage, connect, and inspire this powerful community to excel.

For the culture of care to germinate and evolve, it requires a deep level of commitment and ethically motivated leaders. The challenge that scares most leaders is the constant counter balancing forces that impact the organisation, commonly referred to as stakeholder interests. So, to establish an ethics of care within the organisation, a simple question can be posed to these guardians of the board table: **how do you best exceed the collective expectations of your stakeholders?** This question requires the organisational hierarchy to satisfy the shareholder's desire for improved enterprise value usually through increased share prices (if we may have the liberty of removing the Friedman*esque* insistence on profits). At the same time, they must yield to the demands of the government, its various laws, and social responsibilities, their decisions must not fall foul of employee and community demands in areas such as inclusivity, gender, environment, modern slavery, and safety. Ultimately, achieving the collective expectations of the stakeholders, adds more to enterprise value than does a positive profit outcome. As Warren Buffet noted, 'It takes 20 years to build a reputation and 5 minutes to ruin it. If you think about that, you'll do things differently'. Adverse impacts on reputation, after all, have seen the demise of countless executives, boards, and enterprise value, result in significant remediation activity. Not surprisingly, diplomacy, compromise, and leadership are critical to achieve the optimal stakeholder collective expectation. And the most effective way to achieve this is by inviting the stakeholders to a round table.

4. SQUARING THE CIRCLE AT THE ROUND TABLE

Having established the benefit of the round table framework, in encouraging stakeholders to discuss the issues and solutions of the day, in a safe, open, and respectful environment, we need to turn our minds to the supporting framework. Primarily, we must accept that the existing hierarchical social, political, and economic schema not only remains, but will still play a significant role in outcomes. However, the gossamer underpinning success in this environment are the virtues of leadership within the culture of care. Layered underneath such a round table is a network of interconnected communities, each operating and engaging within their own round tables, to encourage discourse in a broader and more integrated manner (Fig. 6.1). It is here, under the guidance of the respective virtuous leaders outlined previously that the detail of challenges, opportunities, and additional information are uncovered. In short, this layered round table approach sets the direction in 'squaring the circle' from the carcase of hierarchy into an ethics of care.

Fig. 6.1 The Layered Round Table.

Almost confoundingly, it is the most 'under-valued' of all stakeholders that provides the fuel for this engine of ethical decision making to be powered – the employee. We say undervalued, because organisations have typically thought of the employee within the context of union disruption and wages growth. Recently, through the use of social media, whistleblower frameworks and as a result of collectivisation, we have seen the emergence of the power of the employee to impact organisations (sexual discrimination and culture reviews in mining companies), industries (changing approach to concussion in sports – Gridiron, Australian Rules and soccer), governments (modifications to Victorian Government policy on the casino due to the impact it will have on jobs), and societal behaviours (accelerating the public opposition to the live sheep export trade). The employee is always also a customer, a voter, and a member of society that not only has an opinion, but now also has the technology to be seen and heard.

To empower and engage the employee and incorporate stakeholder thinking, the layered round table framework is invoked to enable more detailed interrogation into segments of a much greater issue, broadening the discourse and revealing its hidden truths. Again, the selection of the virtuous leader is critical, as is the definition of objectives as the layer becomes a minor part of a much larger whole. The framework thrives when there is a cascading membership, whereby a representative for each round table is provided to the layer above and below to ensure understanding and a continuity of information sharing and alignment on scenarios considered. In the end, the deeper an enterprise garners participation in the decision-making process, the greater the connection and collaboration across the respective business units, the deeper business knowledge is embedded, and ultimately, the greater the engagement to the 'bigger picture' that reaches beyond the singular round table or business, but rather, becomes reflective of community demands. The value this generates leads to an outcome that is greater than the sum of the parts.

Organisations will dare to challenge the inefficiency and cost of this integrated decision-making process; however, they are typically quite myopic in their metrics for evaluation. Let's consider some scenarios to understand the benefits that this framework brings to the organisation, beyond the simplistic accounting profit valuation and an over-expectation of speed relating to hierarchical decisions. The often quoted 'time and money' metrics for projects, can be viewed in the poor and even catastrophic decisions made by narcissistic leaders and Boards (CEOcracies) globally. Seeped in an ethical framework, we ought to consider the value of this more protracted, yet detailed form of decision making, and more importantly, the time-horizon of these accrued benefits. The reality is that the value positively multiplies the longer the time frame and opportunity for this to evolve and take form in any given enterprise.

Organisations can broadly agree that leadership is most effectively developed internally, because with that comes a known track record, a network of relationships, a better understanding of the peculiarities of the relevant enterprise, the regulatory framework and the various stakeholders that impact the organisations, inevitably differently, regardless of industry, society, or organisational structure. An integrated round table process develops such internal leadership far more effectively than hierarchical, narcissistic leadership structures. It certainly reflects the intentions Burns (1978) held for a 'transforming leadership as a relationship of mutual stimulation and elevation that converts followers into leaders [and we claim that necessarily] converts leaders into moral agents' (. The organisationally embedded nature of the framework will result in more effective execution of a strategy, resulting in both cost savings and time savings, due to the broader involvement in the process and greater organisational understanding. The process, by its integrated and robust structure, would inevitably consider a greater variety of scenarios and potential risk and opportunities, resulting in less remediation activity once rolled out. Understanding that humans are imperfect and prone to errors, the inevitable enhanced oversight may also reduce shortcomings or failures in the decision-making process, with a lower likelihood of ill-considered plans. The layering approach throughout the organisation will materially enhance employee support and engagement in the process.

The development of humanist and caring leaders, internal relationships and engagement with stakeholders will inevitably make future decision making quicker and likely less escalation of decisions to a smaller set of overworked executives – in short, much better day-to-day decision-making will result, combined with a growth in leaders and organisational confidence. The layered round table is the humane model of leadership to face the challenges confronting us today and tomorrow. The humanist and caring model we have set out certainly satisfies Gallo and Hlupic's (2019) leader with 'a radar that serves to understand what is happening through the organisation but also with a moral compass to direct the organisation in the right direction, guided by ethical choices and responsibilities'.

Whilst difficult to quantify, it is quick and simple to reflect on some of the costs of remediation faced by organisations globally, as a result of less inclusive decision-making processes:

- Deepwater Horizon oil spill in the Gulf of Mexico, saw BP pay dearly for the reckless corporate culture of cost-cutting and excessive risk-taking that caused the spill: more than US$60 billion in criminal and civil penalties, natural resource damages, economic claims, and cleanup costs (Uhlmann, 2020).
- Further reflected across multiple Australian banks and their failure to comply with AUSTRAC reporting requirements. The Federal Court of Australia has today ordered Westpac to pay a $1.3 billion penalty for its breaches of the Anti-Money Laundering and Counter-Terrorism Financing Act 2006 (AML/CTF Act). AUSTRAC CEO Nicole Rose PSM said the outcome today sends a strong statement to Westpac and the financial sectors we regulate that they are obliged by law to take their obligations seriously or significant penalties will be applied (AUSTRAC, 2020). An appropriate technological solution and training programme would have cost a mere percentage of that amount.
- Alternatively, the Vale dam burst in Brazil was 'A bare-bones reservoir of mining waste built on the cheap .... Overlooked warnings of structural problems that could lead to a collapse. Monitoring equipment that had stopped working .... And perhaps above all, a country where a powerful mining industry has been free to act more or less unchecked' (Darlingon, 2019).

The list is long, expensive, and regretful.
The contrast between these cultures is shown in Table 6.1.

Table 6.1 Hierarchical Paternalism Strategy Against Round Table Culture.

Hierarchical Paternalism – Strategy	Round Table – Culture
Exploitative	Nurturing
Grandiose narcissism	Courageous and compassionate leadership
Short-term vision	Long-term vision
CEOcracy	Multidisciplinary
Transactional and pseudo–transformational	Relational and transformational
Economic rationalism and paternalism	*Eudaimonic* with an ethics of care

5. CONCLUSION

Hierarchical organisational frameworks are one of the systems of organisation in all the life around us. They exist across most sectors of our community and beyond. We notice them in the animal kingdom from the dominant lion and his pride to the Queen bee and the intricate workings of her hive. This chain of command can be consistently observed on land, in sea, and in air, and oftentimes with the intricate layering of social structures, even within the smallest of creatures. Hierarchical structures are certainly not the only organisational system, but they certainly have come to prominence within the way we humans have organised our society and communities and are quick to recognise in others. We could argue that the hierarchical, systematised, impersonal, and transactional interactions of military and corporate organisational structures which have largely continued to reflect Max Weber's bureaucratic theory of management mirror the natural world around us. The Friedman*esque* hierarchy at the boardroom table is largely characterised by the almost 'blind adherence' to policies and procedures, standardised processes, number of desks (albeit in possibly open-plan offices), meticulous divisions of labour, clear hierarchies, and professional, almost impersonal interactions between employees. However, we argue that this vision is too singular in its aims and does not reflect the complexities of our social or personal needs at the most intrinsic level. During the most recent pandemic, CEOs and academics have come together to rethink the kind of leadership we need to face the onslaught of new crises we can identify as the 4thIR. In this chapter, we have attempted to address this call to arms for humane leadership motivated by ethical decision making. We have offered a reimagining of this hierarchy which encourages the expression and interaction of the changing cultural and environmental nuances of a fast-changing world. Inspired by our own humanity, we have proposed a layered round table framework nestled in an ethics of care. We have proposed a process of engagement, under a virtuous leader, that is founded on humane interaction courage and respect. A leader with Aristotelian virtues conducting a round table that enables broader consideration, participation, respectful opinion, and discourse that is built upon an ethics of care. For humanity to flourish well into tomorrow, we must redefine leadership, engage better, and make decisions not just for the individual, but for our communities too.

REFERENCES

Alston, M., & Whittenbury, K. (Eds.). (2013). *Research, action and policy: Addressing the gendered impact of climate change*. Springer.

Akrivou, K., Bourantas, D., Mo, S., & Papalois, E. (2011). The sound of silence – A space for morality? The role of solitude for ethical decision making. *Journal of Business Ethics*, *102*(1), 119–133.

Al-Shammari, M., Rasheed, A., & Al-Shammari, H. A. (2019). CEO narcissism and corporate social responsibility: Does CEO narcissism affect CSR focus?*Journal of Business Research*, *104*, 106–117.

Asbari, M. (2020). Is transformational leadership suitable for future organizational needs?*International Journal of Sociology, Policy and Law*, *1*(1), 51–55.

AUSTRAC. (2020). Westpac ordered to pay $1.3 billion penalty. Australian Government.

Bass, B. M., & Avolio, B. J. (1994). Transformational leadership and organizational culture. *International Journal of Public Administration*, *17*, 541–554.

Borgerson, J. (2007). On the harmony of feminist ethics and business ethics. *Business and Society Review*, *112*(4), 477–509.

Bossi, L. (2023). How a sense of place may return the social license to operate concept back to an ethics of responsibility within a neoliberal framework—A Tasmanian Salmon story. *Research in Ethical Organisations*, *27*, 25–46.

Bragues, G. (2006). Seek the good life, not money: The Aristotelian approach to business ethics. *Journal of Business Ethics*, *67*(4), 341–357.

Brown, M. E., & Treviño, L. K. (2006). Ethical leadership: A review and future directions. *The Leadership Quarterly*, *17*(6), 595–616.

Burns, J. M. (1978). *Leadership/James MacGregor burns*. Harper & Row.

Buyl, T., Boone, C., & Wade, J. B. (2019). CEO narcissism, risk-taking, and resilience: An empirical analysis in U.S. commercial banks. *Journal of Management*, *45*(4), 1372–1400.

Caggiano, V., & Ragusa, A. (2022). Leadership and emotions. Lessons from Sant'Ignazio de Loyola and Martha Nussbaum. *Studi sulla Formazione*, *25*(2), 123.

Cingöz, A., & Akdoğan, A. A. (2019). A study on determining the relationships among corporate social responsibility, organizational citizenship behavior and ethical leadership. *International Journal of Innovation and Technology Management*, *16*(04), 1940004.

Darlingon, S. (2019, January 25). 7 people killed and 200 missing in Brazil after dam collapses, officials say. *The New York Times*. Retrieved from https://www.nytimes.com/2019/01/25/world/americas/brazil-dam-burst-brumadinho.html.

DeYoung, R., Peng, E. Y., & Yan, M. (2013). Executive compensation and business policy choices at U.S. commercial banks. *Journal of Financial & Quantitative Analysis*, *48*(1), 165–196.

Doehner, W., Mazighi, M., Hofmann, B. M., Lautsch, D., Hindricks, G., Bohula, E. A., Byrne, R. A., Camm, A. J., Casadei, B., Caso, V., Cognard, C., Diener, H.-C., Endres, M., Goldstein, P., Halliday, A., Hopewell, J. C., Jovanovic, D. R., Kobayashi, A., Kostrubiec, M., ... Widimsky, P. (2020). Cardiovascular care of patients with stroke and high risk of stroke: The need for interdisciplinary action. A consensus report from the European Society of Cardiology Cardiovascular Round Table. *European Journal of Preventive Cardiology*, *27*(7), 682–692.

Drucker, P. (1954). *The practice of management* (pp. 1–416). Harper Business.

Elliott, P., Cowie, M. R., Franke, J., Ziegler, A., Antoniades, C., Bax, J., Bucciarelli-Ducci, C., Flachskampf, F. A., Hamm, C., Jensen, M. T., Katus, H., Maisel, A., McDonagh, T., Mittmann, C., Muntendam, P., Nagel, E., Rosano, G., Twerenbold, R., & Zannad, F. (2020). Development, validation, and implementation of biomarker testing in cardiovascular medicine state-of-the-art: Proceedings of the European Society of Cardiology—Cardiovascular Round Table. *Cardiovascular Research*, *117*(5), 1248–1256.

Ellis, B. (2011). Humanism and morality. *Sophia*, *50*(1), 135–139.

Erba, P. A., Habib, G., Glaudemans, A. W. J. M., Miro, J. M., & Slart, R. H. J. A. (2017). The round table approach in infective endocarditis & cardiovascular implantable electronic devices infections: Make your e-Team come true. *European Journal of Nuclear Medicine and Molecular Imaging*, *44*(7), 1107–1108.

Friedman, M. (1962). *Capitalism and freedom*. University of Chicago Press.

Gallo, P., & Hlupic, W. (2019). *Humane leadership must be the Fourth Industrial Revolution's real innovation.* https://www.weforum.org/agenda/2019/05/humane-leadership-is-the-4irs-big-management-innovation/

Gilligan, C. (1982). *In a different voice: Psychological theory and women's development* (pp. 1–184). Harvard University Press.

Grethlein, J. (2012). Xenophon's "Anabasis" from character to narrator. *The Journal of Hellenic Studies, 132*, 23–40.

Hermalin, B. E. (1999, April). *Economic and corporate culture.* https://ssrn.com/abstract=162549 or http://dx.doi.org/10.2139/ssrn.162549

Hermalin, B. E. (2012). Leadership and corporate culture. In R. Gibbons & J. Roberts (Eds.), *The handbook of organizational economics* (pp. 432–478). Princeton University Press.

Howland, J. (2000). Xenophon's philosophic Odyssey: On the Anabasis and Plato's Republic. *American Political Science Review, 94*(4), 875–889.

Humphreys, J. H., & Einstein, W. O. (2003). Nothing new under the sun: Transformational leadership from a historical perspective. *Management Decision, 41*, 85–95.

Institute of Medicine (IOM) Roundtable on Evidence-based Medicine. (2007). *The learning healthcare system: Workshop summary.* National Academies Press.

Jia, Y., Chen, O., Xiao, Z., Xiao, J., Bian, J., & Jia, H. (2020). Nurses' ethical challenges caring for people with COVID-19: A qualitative study. *Nursing Ethics, 28*(1), 33–45.

Kalshoven, K., Hartog, D. N. N., & Hoogh, A. H. B. D. (2011). Ethical leadership at work questionnaire (ELW): Development and validation of a multidimensional measure. *The Leadership Quarterly, 22*(1), 51–69.

Kang, S. W. (2019). Sustainable influence of ethical leadership on work performance: Empirical study of multinational enterprise in South Korea. *Sustainability, 11*(11), 3101.

Kristinsson, K., Stangej, O., Sund, B., & Minelgaite, I. (2024). Does gender matter in ethical leadership perceptions? Cross-national evidence. *Economics & Sociology, 17*(1), 236–255.

Law, S. (2011). *Humanism: A very short introduction* [ebook]. Oxford University Press.

Leclercq, C., Witt, H., Hindricks, G., Katra, R. P., Albert, D., Belliger, A., Cowie, M. R., Deneke, T., Friedman, P., Haschemi, M., Lobban, T., Lordereau, I., McConnell, M. V., Rapallini, L., Samset, E., Turakhia, M. P., Singh, J. P., Svennberg, E., Wadhwa, M., & Weidinger, F. (2022). Wearables, telemedicine, and artificial intelligence in arrhythmias and heart failure: Proceedings of the European Society of Cardiology Cardiovascular Round Table. *EP Europace, 24*(9), 1372–1383.

Lee, L. C., & Hoe, L. C. (2022). Fostering individual ethical behaviour through integrated corporate social responsibility and ethical leadership. *International Journal of Research Publications, 104*(1), 514–554.

Levine, M. P., & Boaks, J. (2014). What does ethics have to do with leadership? *Journal of Business Ethics, 124*, 225–242.

Liveris, C. (2022). Mining industry must stay committed to weeding out sex creeps. The West Australian. Retrieved from https://thewest.com.au/opinion/conrad-liveris-resources-industry-must-stay-committed-to-weeding-out-sex-creeps-c-7633071.

Maiden, S. (2021, March 9). *Liberal MPs respond to Julie Bishop's 'big swinging dicks' claim.* Retrieved from https://www.news.com.au/national/politics/julie-bishop-launches-extraordinary-attack-on-canberra-culture/news-story/f24ee2a3d4d08af42dde5895ee9e5077.

Malmendier, U., & Tate, G. (2005). CEO overconfidence and corporate investment. *The Journal of Finance, 60*, 2661–2700.

Nussbaum, M. (1992). *Love's knowledge: Essays on philosophy and literature* (pp. 1–404). Oxford University Press.

O'Reilly, C. A., & Chatman, J. A. (2020). Transformational leader or narcissist? How grandiose narcissists can create and destroy organizations and institutions. *California Management Review, 62*(3), 5–27.

Pini, M. (2021, March 11). Big swinging dicks and the rule of law. Retrieved from https://independentaustralia.net/politics/politics-display/big-swinging-dicks-and-the-rule-of-law,14882.

Reiner, R. (1992). *A few good men* (138 minutes). Columbia Pictures.

Sankowsky, D. (1995). The charismatic leader as narcissist: Understanding the abuse of power. *Organizational Dynamics, 23*(4), 57–71.

Scott, R. H. (2011). The financial crisis inquiry report: Final report of the National Commission on the causes of the financial and economic crisis in the United States. *American Library Association CHOICE, 48*, 2368.

The International Council on Monuments and Sites. (2023). *Australia ICOMOS*. https://australia.icomos.org/resources/burra-charter-series/

Uhlmann, D. M. (2020, April 23). BP paid a steep price for the Gulf oil spill but for the US a decade later, it's business as usual. *The Conversation*. Retrieved from https://theconversation.com/bp-paid-a-steep-price-for-the-gulf-oil-spill-but-for-the-us-a-decade-later-its-business-as-usual-136905.

Walumbwa, F. O., Avolio, B. J., Gardner, W. L., Wernsing, T. S., & Peterson, S. J. (2007). Authentic leadership: Development and validation of a theory-based measure. *Journal of Management, 34*(1), 89–126.

Weber, M. (1922). *Economy and society*. Bedminster.

White, N. (2019). *From shipwreck to shipshape: The incredible story of PTC's boardroom table*. https://www.ptc.com/ en/blogs/corporate/121-seaport-shipwreck-boardroom

Wu, M. (2017). *Seaport shipwreck*. Archaeology. City of Boston. Retrieved from https://www.boston.gov/departments/archaeology/seaport-shipwreck.

BOOK REVIEWS

CHAPTER 7

BOOK REVIEW: MARTHA NUSSBAUM'S *JUSTICE FOR ANIMALS: OUR COLLECTIVE RESPONSIBILITY*

Jacqueline Boaks

Curtin University, Australia

ABSTRACT

Martha Nussbaum's Justice for Animals: Our Collective Responsibility *is a profound exploration of the ethical obligations humans owe to non-human animals, arguing that humanity's stewardship role encompasses even the wildest creatures. The book is a blend of philosophical discourse, scientific insights on animal sentience, and personal reflections, grounded in the author's deep engagement with animal ethics. Central to the author's argument is the idea that animals deserve justice, which Nussbaum defines as the prevention of wrongful thwarting of their significant striving, emphasising that the injustice towards animals is not merely about preventing pain but respecting their capabilities and characteristic forms of life. The author critiques existing approaches to animal rights, such as utilitarianism and species hierarchy, advocating instead for her capabilities approach. This approach posits that animals should have opportunities to flourish according to their nature, and even calls for radical ideas like animals having advocates in legislative processes. The author's work is marked by a moral urgency, arguing that our increasing knowledge of animal sentience demands that we take their suffering seriously. The author also addresses complex ethical issues like the morality of meat eating and the ethical treatment of wild animals, concluding with a hopeful outlook on the potential for significant political and legal advancements in animal justice. Despite its ambitious scope, the book is a compelling call to rethink our ethical responsibilities towards animals.*

Keywords: Animal ethics; animal rights; justice; Nussbaum; capabilities approach

BOOK DETAILS

Nussbaum, M. C. (2022). Justice for animals: Our collective responsibility (First Simon & Schuster hardcover edition). Simon & Schuster. 372 pages. ISBN: 9781982102500, 9781982102517, 1982102500, 1982102519 Trade Paperback/eBook $18.99/$13.99

Martha Nussbaum's latest book, *Justice for Animals: Our Collective Responsibility* raises the ethical issues that arise from our treatment of animals across the entire spectrum of our interactions with them. Or better, the book addresses what we owe to non-human animals throughout their entire existence. Nussbaum argues that humans have an increasingly hard to deny 'stewardship' role over even the 'wildest' animals and environments.

The book itself is an ambitious mix of philosophical argument, despatches from the field of the latest scientific research on animal sentience and capabilities, and personal reflections. Its central thesis is a call to arms to appreciate and redress the current significant and pervasive injustices towards non-human animals.

From the beginning, Nussbaum takes seriously the consideration of what we morally owe to non-human animals, engages deeply and admirably with the serious philosophical and animal science thinking in this area, and offers an undeniably personal and even biographical approach to these topics.

For Nussbaum, the origins of her connection to the topic are personal and one cannot help but be touched by her account of coming to the topic clearly through her beloved late daughter's passion and career in the field.

The book starts with a call to attention that is marked by amoral clarity and sense of urgency that is remarkable even among so many of the now common calls to action and alarm on human impact on the natural world. This call to attention draws on the undeniable twin claims that the level of human impact has dramatically increased in recent decades along with the number of us who are implicated in the suffering this causes to non-human animals and that this suffering is well documented. Nussbaum argues convincingly that the increase in our knowledge of animals and their lives means we are no longer in a position (if we ever were) to hold that animals are creatures 'without a subjective sense of the world, without emotions, without society, and perhaps even without the feeling of pain' (p. 8).

Nussbaum is clear that her focus is the status of individual animals. While she is not unconcerned with the extinction of animal species, her primary focus is suffering and the injustice she takes this to represent. As she notes though, 'extinction never takes place without massive suffering of individual creatures' (p. 5).

The other element that is explicit from the start is Nussbaum's advocacy of emotion in motivating our response to the suffering of animals and the injustice that she argues this represents. Throughout the book, the argument is grounded in and motivated by an emotive response to animals, their lives, and (central to her own capabilities approach) their abilities.

For Nussbaum, these appropriate emotions are tied together. They fit into both Aristotle's views of the role between emotions and morality and her own capabilities approach and lead us from recognition of the wrongs of these injustices towards motivation to act to redress them (p. 28). The emotions Nussbaum aims to promote in her readers are specifically: 'a sense of ethically attuned wonder that might lead to an ethically directed compassion when the animal's striving is wrongfully thwarted, and a forward-looking outrage that says: "This is unacceptable. It must not happen again"' (p. 28).

For Nussbaum, 'injustice centrally involves significant striving blocked by not just harm but also wrongful thwarting, whether negligent or deliberate. Often, thwarting includes the infliction of pain, which impedes almost every ordinary activity of an organism (perceiving, eating, moving, loving)' (p. 26). Nussbaum herself acknowledges that in offering such a definition she is 'going down to the bedrock intuitions of my theory, where it is really very hard to give further reasons' (p. 23).

The subsequent sections of the book explore and despatch what Nussbaum argues are the contemporary and dominant attempts to achieve increased moral standing and legal protection for animals.

These begin with approaches that arrange animals in a hierarchy of animal species from least to most human what Nussbaum refers to as the 'so like us' model. Clearly, this approach has achieved advances in treatment for some animals, including legal personhood for chimpanzees and other primates, but Nussbaum rejects as unjustified its focus on those abilities that closely match those of humans and argues that it reinforces the hierarchical thinking that has caused such disregard for animal suffering.

Utilitarian approaches also fall short, according to Nussbaum, because

> although pain is very important, and ending gratuitous pain is an urgent goal, animals are agents, and their lives have other relevant aspects: dignity, social capacity, curiosity, play, planning, and free movement among others. Their flourishing is best conceived in terms of opportunities for choice of activities, not just states of satisfaction.

While reserving perhaps her strongest admiration for Christine Korsgaard's recent Kantian approaches to animal rights, she nonetheless rejects what she sees as too sharp a division between humans and animals on this view, including on the question of animals as moral agents (contra Korsgaard, Nussbaum argues that animals such as dogs do have some moral capacity such as 'When a dog heroically saves a drowning child' they are 'performing acts of altruism and treating other creatures as ends', p. 89).

Chapter 5 introduces Nussbaum's by now well-known 'capabilities approach' and outlines how it might apply to animals. Making a nuanced and clear connection with Rawls and with the shortcomings of models of economic development that she argues do not pay sufficient weight to the dignity and interest of individual humans over the aggregate well-being, Nussbaum extends this to the capabilities that animals have. The capabilities approach, she argues, also gives us the basis for a model of justice for animals that turns on them having a characteristic way of life and rights and interests in this not being thwarted.

Here the book quickly becomes relatively radical in its early proposals – for example, that animals deserve to 'participate actively in legislation and institution-building' (p. 111) albeit through advocates and collaborators.

> The ideal outcome would be for all the nations of the world (listening astutely to the demands of animals and those who most knowledgeably represent them) to agree to a legally enforceable constitution for the various animal species, each with its own list of capabilities to be protected, and each supplied with a threshold level beneath which non-protection becomes injustice. Animals would then be protected no matter where they are, just as whales are (inadequately) protected all over the world by the IWC. (p. 113)

As an exemplar of where Nussbaum thinks we should be headed, she cites a 2016 US Ninth Circuit Court ruling protecting whales, upholding their right to their way of life over the US Navy's wish to use sonar. Nussbaum sees it as a case where human advocates were motivated by the afore-mentioned 'wonder' at the whales' capabilities and a consequent desire to protect them (pp. 128–129).

Chapter 6 ('Sentience and Striving') connects many of these threads and sees Nussbaum begin to identify which animals fall within the domain of justice – that is, if justice involves thwarting of significant striving, then what are the necessary conditions of such striving? Nussbaum identifies three from the literature: apprehension of what is harmful to the animal, subjective sensory awareness, and a sense of significance regarding external elements and outcomes (p. 138). Without these three, Nussbaum, argues, the 'significant striving' that is central to her theory of justice cannot be present (p. 140). Having established this as the principle, Nussbaum turns to the empirical evidence to come to some conclusions about where that boundary sits, noting that many of these conclusions are speculative. Mammals are taken as a given since it seems 'obvious' to Nussbaum that the scientific consensus laid out so far makes it clear that they possess the necessary attributes for this significant striving (p. 151). Some cases are obvious (insects and sponges are out, octopuses are in), some less so (bees may show the necessary attributes). In other cases (e.g. hermit crabs), Nussbaum concludes that the evidence is inconclusive and that we should err on the side of caution. Those creatures that do qualify have a justice claim on us – that is, we do not interfere with the creature's ability 'to flourish in its own way' (p. 162). Here, the claims of justice are neatly stated, but the language has shifted from striving to flourishing.

Chapter 7 moves on to consider the 'the harm of death' and seeks to show that a satisfactory philosophical investigation into the harm of death, combined with the capabilities approach, leads us away from both the classic utilitarian view (that a painless death for human needs is sometimes morally acceptable) and the animal rights view (that it is always wrong to kill an animal for human needs) (pp. 164–165). This serious philosophical examination begins with an exploration of the dominant philosophical thinking on whether and how death is a harm to humans (indeed half the chapter is spent on this). Nussbaum lands on the interruption argument – that death harms us because it 'interrupts' the flow and shape of our lives (p. 173). For Nussbaum 'the heart of the matter' is that meat eating is the cause of most animal deaths caused by humans currently and that the majority of these are animals such as pigs, cows, birds, and fish. All these animals have been established, in the previous chapter, as ones who display the kind of sentience and striving that mean we owe them justice and for whom the interruption argument therefore applies. Animals with no temporal sense, such as some fish, are clearly then not candidates for this kind of harm (p. 177). Here, Nussbaum concludes that those like her who eat fish for their own nutrition are not therefore committing any serious moral wrong, though she acknowledges the moral peril of human beings 'judge and jury in our own case' here (p. 179). Here, Nussbaum advocates a progressivist approach, acknowledging as well that there are wealth and access differences in one's ability to transition away from a diet that includes animals who are harmed by their deaths (and lives) (p. 181).

Following on from the introduction of this ethical complexity, Chapter 8 considers so-called 'tragic dilemmas'. This chapter too, starts with an overview of the current philosophical approaches to tragic dilemmas before offering Nussbaum's own original views on this and applying this to the question of justice and animals. This is another sign of what a serious question of justice Nussbaum treats this as. The work is a serious discussion of justice *qua* justice. Here, Nussbaum follows Hegel and his suggestion that the wise course of action is to look for ways we can prevent future tragic dilemmas, even while acknowledging this is not always possible (p. 184). Government policy and social structures have a role to play in avoiding these tragic dilemmas, and here Nussbaum draws on her knowledge of these to illustrate examples from the development sector, before applying these ideas to the question of medical research on animals and how we might transition to replacing these methods and what principles the capabilities approach will dictate for animal treatment between now and then. Nussbaum then returns to 'meat eating again' (p. 192) arguing the 'Hegelian solution' is artificial meat, then rejecting most claims to preserve harmful treatment of animals made on the basis of 'cultural preservation'. This last point sees Nussbaum on perhaps the least firm ground and some will find her views that are less than well supported or hard to stomach, even before the suggestion that 'it is likely that the values involved in Nazism were deeply woven into German cultural traditions' before heralding the German move away from Nazism as a positive case of a culture surviving such a change (p. 195).

The final considerations in the chapter – 'conflicts over space and resources' – Nussbaum acknowledges are 'far more tenacious' (p. 197) and the solutions discussed are similarly more hard bitten – not just animal reserves and increasing the rule of law to prevent poaching but also human population control as well as animal contraceptives (p. 199). Here too, Nussbaum advocates for a Hegelian approach that considers 'what we might do to produce a future world in which that grim choice does not arise' (p. 200).

Chapter 9 addresses companion animals, focussing largely on cats and dogs. While noting that the dependent and vulnerable situation of most companion animals is regrettable, nonetheless Nussbaum is not an abolitionist about companion animals. Instead, the capabilities approach is explored to note what rights these animals have, and Nussbaum's preferred solution is a form of citizenship for these animals that brings with it regulatory protection and collective responsibilities towards them. Nussbaum endorses legal standing for animals, though not citizenship of the same kind as humans, as well as an argument that many of the most popular breeds of dogs live such unhealthy lives as to make their continued breeding morally impermissible. Here, the comparisons between the state of animals and those with a disability as well as with slaves of the past are often thoughtful and well-drawn but may nonetheless be objectionable to some.

Chapter 10 naturally enough moves on to what we commonly call 'wild animals'. To some extent, Nussbaum's views are summed up in the sub-heading we find partway through the chapter: 'The 'Wild' Is Not Good and It Does Not Exist Anyway' (p. 233). Rejecting the common arguments that human intervention in wild spaces and the lives of wild animals will always be ill-informed or paternalistic, Nussbaum argues that humans already undeniably and heavily influence wild spaces. Thus, stewardship is the only option. Ultimately, over and above some nuanced discussion of specific, Nussbaum offers the relatively undeniable conclusion that 'typically the measures that protect animal habitats in general are good for all the animals in those habitats' (p. 241) and that in many instances and in many of their current forms zoos are ethically impermissible (i.e. where it precludes the animal's 'characteristic form of life' p. 547). Predation is morally permissible to continue even under stewardship where it is part of some animals' characteristics form of life (p. 253) and not, for example, the result of introduced species (p. 255) but the circumstances are different in the case of domestic cats and the suffering it would cause to allow them to prey on small animals and birds (pp. 252–253).

Chapter 11 addresses 'the capabilities of friendship'. Here, the book tells rather sensitively and often beautifully stories of what Nussbaum takes to be genuine friendship between humans and animals (companion animals, wild animals, and captive animals). The elements of 'wonder' and empathy return here, and Nussbaum makes the case that this is true friendship, not just 'affiliation' as per the capabilities approach. Here too, as well as a grounding in the philosophical literature on what friendship is, there is a focus on respect for the animal's characteristic form of life as central and necessary.

Chapter 12 is 'The Role of Law'. 'The idea of a virtual constitution is just a metaphor, in the absence of institutions that can enforce those rights' (p. 282). But as she notes, if we lack global enforceability of human rights, how much more so for animals in the absence of global consensus (and animals 'belong' to states in far less ways than humans do). Nussbaum lays out a kind of audit of existing laws in this area, mostly in the USA, convincingly arguing that we are not starting from nothing in this area. 'Each of these laws has serious gaps and flaws, but with all their deficiencies, the federal and state laws we currently have offer a surprising amount of protection to at least some animals' (p. 290).

Here, Nussbaum identifies two main issues – animals lack legal standing (so others cannot act on their behalf) (p. 291), and the imperfect laws that do apply here have led to mostly failed efforts. Nussbaum thinks a better option than addressing these flaws and following this path is pursuing fiduciary law (p. 295). 'And this approach fits particularly well with the capabilities approach: fiduciary law is not just concerned with avoiding pain or even harm to the beneficiary, but rather with actively advancing the beneficiary's interests in a broad way' (p. 296). Ultimately, as Nussbaum, notes, the solution requires increasing human consciousness of – and motivation towards – addressing justice for animals, which will be the animating force to improve laws and enforcement of this justice.

The conclusion ends the book on a hopeful note. Nussbaum reflects that 'Ours is a time of a great awakening: to our kinship with a world of remarkable intelligent creatures, and to real accountability for our treatment of them' (p. 315). One need not agree with Nussbaum that her capabilities approach is best placed to support and further this awakening to hope she is right in predicting that the 'concrete political developments' towards animal justice that the conclusion outlines will continue.

Increasingly these are issues faced in areas of practical ethics as well as in organisations ranging from the testing of products on animals, the farming of animals for meat and food, and the impact on wild animals and their habitats whether directly or indirectly. It follows convincingly from Nussbaum's argument that even organisations with no direct involvement in the former can hardly deny their impact on the latter. The impact of climate change on animal species has sharpened the sense in which this is indeed a 'collective responsibility' that the title of this book refers to.

It is interesting and compelling to read such a capable philosopher navigate the ground between political and moral philosophy and broader topics including accounts of advances in what science is telling us about the capabilities and sentience of animals and do so in the service of what is a clear moral demand on all of us.

Nussbaum rapidly strips away any moral pretence or superiority the reader might feel about their own choices in this area. By page 2, for example, any sense of moral comfort that one might have from conscientious choices such as a plant-based diet is neatly despatched.

This blending of these elements is an ambitious task. At times such an approach risks not doing justice to any of the individual areas.

Relatedly, it can be hard to decide exactly what the intended audience of the book is. When it comes to the philosophical argument, for example, there are places where a philosophical reader could wish for at once less introductory background on such well-known theories such as Bentham's utilitarian ethics and the foundations of Kantian ethics, and at the same time more in-depth philosophical argument. For example, in places it is not clear why we should not think a revised sentience theory such as that of Bentham (which Nussbaum refers to) might not provide us with all of the justice claims that Nussbaum's capabilities approach does.

On the other hand, the use of 'justice' can seem question begging if the audience does not already accept the capabilities approach (the argument for which does not come until rather late in the book). The start of the book, for example, is at pains to ground 'injustice' as the thwarting of 'significant striving' on behalf of the animal in question. But it is not clear to the reader why we should not simply consider this 'wrongful thwarting' as a synonym for injustice. On the other hand, Nussbaum does not always sufficiently address the obvious point that significant harm (injustice) can be done to an animal even in the absence of this striving. Bare sentience seems to give enough scope that pain and harm appear to be a serious injustice. And it does no good to simply state that thwarting significant strivings is a greater injustice – this risks being either question begging or stipulative. Nussbaum does engage with these other questions regarding these dominant theories, but the answers may not satisfy all readers.

Similarly, to the non-philosophical reader, the book might often read as too philosophical and too concerned with the finer ethical grounding that in places Nussbaum notes results in these same justice claims.

Perhaps related to this is the fact that at times the reader would be forgiven for being unclear whether the book is a defence of the capabilities approach or a simple application of it. At times, largely when engaging with and criticising what Nussbaum sees as three main alternatives to the capabilities approach (the 'so like us approach', Kantian approaches such as those of Christine Korsgaard, and utilitarian approaches from Bentham to Singer), she offers an argument for the capabilities approach as best placed to explain what we owe to animals or current progress (or perhaps intuitions), at other times an argument for animal treatment changes based on the capabilities approach.

The scope and structure of the book also raise the role of moral intuitions in such arguments. The book begins and ends with an appeal to a sense of 'wonder, awe, and outrage' – wonder and awe regarding the capabilities of non-human animals and what Nussbaum describes as legitimate and useful anger at their current treatment and sufferings. What would have been gained or lost by stopping with that appeal to intuition? Indeed, it is hard not to share what Nussbaum describes as a useful and rightful anger on behalf of these animals and the injustices done to them by our own species. Throughout, the book moves back and forth between such appeals to intuition largely in the form of compassion (no bad thing) and philosophical argument to ground the justice claims of animals.

There is also the risk of being overly optimistic when the book takes what Nussbaum describes as the Hegelian approach to tragic dilemmas or conflicts between the interests of wild animals and humans – more evidence is needed to convince us that many of these tragic conflicts between the interests of humans and non-human animals can be engineered away (whether we take 'can' in the sense of possible or likely to happen given our current political and economic arrangements). The proposal for offices overseeing domestic animal welfare seems plausible, intervening in some predation in the wild less so.

Some of the comparisons between the treatment of women, slaves, people with a disability, and animals certainly risk being insensitive. The responses here can be read as rushed and lacking nuance. For example, when Nussbaum notes 'pushback' on animal rights advocates who compare the treatment of non-human animals and slavery, she claims that this is 'presumably because it can be read as suggesting, inappropriately, that African Americans are like chimps' (pp. 46–47). But this seems a strange reading of what might be offensive about such a comparison. Even given the uncontroversial assumption that there is something that makes it wrong to keep chimpanzees in the conditions they are often kept in is compatible with the idea that there might be something uniquely egregious about keeping (any) humans as slaves.

Nonetheless, in addition to the valuable contribution it makes to an important ethical debate, the book is worthwhile and intellectually compelling not despite but because of this ambition. In addition to its being a welcome addition to the increasing calls for better treatment of animals, it is worthwhile watching a philosopher of this stature and command of her field attempting such an ambitious task. If there are parts where the reader might wish for more focus on the philosophy, the science, the moral intuitions, or a different combination of them, this is largely a reflection of the difficulty of such a task. It is interesting and informative to observe such a skilled philosopher attempt to construct a philosophical work that appeals to our well-held intuitions and our better selves in the form of a serious call to action across such a large range of human activities.

REFERENCE

Nussbaum, M. C. (2022). *Justice for animals: Our collective responsibility* (First Simon & Schuster hardcover ed.). Simon & Schuster.

www.ingramcontent.com/pod-product-compliance
Lightning Source LLC
Jackson TN
JSHW060717090725
87332JS00004B/131